Listening to Reading

Listening to Reading

Stephen Ratcliffe

State University of New York Press

Cover illustration:
Oona Ratcliffe, "Color Study,"
1998, Paper Collage,
4 ½″ × 3 ½″, Private Collection.

Published by
State University of New York Press, Albany

Printed in the United States of America

For information, address State University of New York Press
State University Plaza, Alabany, New York 12246

Production by Dana Foote
Marketing by Patrick Durocher

Library of Congress Cataloging-in-Publication Data

Ratcliffe, Stephen.
Listening to reading / Stephen Ratcliffe.
p. cm.
A collection of essays written 1985–1998 for various occasions and published, many in earlier versions, in various sources, 1986–1999.
Includes bibliographical references and index.
ISBN 0–7914–4503–8 (hc : alk. paper)—ISBN 0–7914–4504–6 (pb : alk. paper)
1. American poetry—20th century—History and criticism. 2. Experimental poetry, American—History and criticism. 3. Mallarmâ, Stâphane, 1842–1898—Influence. 4. Visual poetry—History and criticism. 5. Sound poetry—History and criticism. 6. Oral interpretation of poetry. I. Title.
PS325 .R38 2000
811′.509—dc21 99–088760

10 9 8 7 6 5 4 3 2 1

for
Robert Grenier

Contents

Illustrations

Acknowledgments

The essays collected here were written between 1985 and 1998 for various occasions and have appeared, often in substantively earlier versions, in the following publications and contexts. My thanks to the editors for their support of my work.

"Con(   )Text": *Witz,* ed. Chris Reiner (vol. 1, no. 1, 1992).

"The Asymptote of Elsewhere": *Peninsula,* ed. Joe Safdie (no. 4, 1991). Presented at a Faculty Seminar at Mills College on November 30, 1987.

"Echoes": *Conjunctions,* ed. Bradford Morrow (no. 16, Winter 1991). Presented at the Edward de Vere Studies Conference, Concordia University, Portland, OR, on April 4, 1998.

"Writing [Echoes] Writing": *Santa Barbara Review,* ed. Patricia Stockton Leddy (vol. 2, no. 1, 1994); portions also appeared in *Texture* (no. 5, 1993), *exposures* (no. 3, 1993) and *amnesia* (Texture Chapbook Series no. 8, 1993), all edited by Susan Smith Nash. Presented at the Bay Area Writers Workshop, at Mills College, on August 7, 1989.

"Notes on Sound": *Temblor,* ed. Leland Hickman (no. 10, 1989). Presented at the Bay Area Writers Workshop, at Mills College, on August 2, 1988.

"Memo/ Re: Reading Stein": *American Poetry,* ed. Lee Bartlett (no. 6, 1989). Presented as a talk at Mills College on December 8, 1987.

"Reading (Cage) *Silence*": *corner* (no. 3, 2000); Presented at "Here Comes Everybody: The Music, Poetry, and Art of John Cage," Mills College, November 16, 1995.

"Writing/ Re: Memory/ I": *American Poetry* ed. Lee Bartlett (vol. 4, no. 3, 1987). Presented at the NEH Summer Institute Studies in Modern Poetry at New York University, August 1985; also presented as a talk at Mills College on February 23, 1987.

"Writing/ Re: Memory/ II and III": *Temblor,* ed. Leland Hickman (no. 6, 1986).

"Signature": portions of this work appeared in *Object,* ed. Rob Fitterman and Kim Rosenfield (no. 2, 1993); *Anthology of North American Ideophonics,* ed. Mark Nowak (no. 1, 1993); *Anabasis,* ed. Thomas Taylor (no. 2, 1993); *Talisman,* ed. Edward Foster (no. 12, 1994); *Re*Map,* ed. Todd Baron and Carolyn Kemp (no. 5, 1996); and *First Intensity,* ed. Lee Chapman (vol. 5, no. 2, 1998).

"Grenier's 'Scrawl'": *Witz,* ed. Chris Reiner (1996).

"Mallarmé: poem in prose": *Poetic Briefs,* ed. Elizabeth Burns and Jefferson Hansen (no. 18, 1994); reprinted in *Santa Barbara Review,* ed. Patricia Stockton Leddy (vol. 3, no. 3, 1995); also reprinted as "Preface" to *Mallarmé: poem in prose* (Santa Barbara Review Press, 1998).

"Listening to Reading/ I": *Poetics Journal,* ed. Barrett Watten and Lyn Hejinian (no. 6, 1986).

"Listening to Reading/ II": *Temblor,* ed. Leland Hickman (no. 8, 1988).

"Listening to Reading/ III": *Talisman,* ed. Leland Hickman (no. 8, 1992).
"Sound (Shape) as Thought": *Furnitures,* ed. Mark Nowak (no. 7, 1992).
"Eigner's 'Scores'": *Witz,* ed. Chris Reiner (vol. 5, no. 1, 1997) and *Shadow Play,* ed. John Martone (no. 5, 1997). Presented at memorial readings for Larry Eigner at University of California at Berkeley on April 10, 1996, and June 15, 1997.
"Idea's Mirror/ I": *The Difficulties,* ed. Tom Beckett (vol. 3, no. 2, 1989).
"Idea's Mirror/ II": *Talisman,* ed. Edward Foster (no. 4, 1990).
"Utter Mimesis": *Occident,* ed. P. Michael Campbell (vol. 103, no. 3, 1990).
"Writing *A Reading*": *Raddle Moon 13,* ed. Susan Clark, Catriona Strang, and Lisa Robertson (vol. 6, no. 2, 1995).
"Cracking the Code": *The Difficulties,* ed. Tom Beckett (vol. 3, no. 1, 1987).
"Reading *Sun*": *Occident,* ed. P. Michael Campbell (vol. 103, no. 3, 1990).
"Supernatural Duet": *Talisman,* ed. Edward Foster (no. 7, Fall 1991).
"Axis of Simultaneities": *The Poetry Project Newsletter,* ed. Jerome Sala (no. 141, 1991).
"The Landscape (Body) of the Poem": portions of this work appeared in "Patterns/Context/Time: A Symposium on Contemporary Poetry": *Tyuonyi,* ed. Phillip Foss and Charles Bernstein (no. 6/7, 1990) and in *anabasis,* ed. Thomas Taylor (no. 1, 1992).

Grateful thanks also to the following people, who read and made valuable comments on portions of this work: Joe Amato, Ulla Dydo, Susan Gevirtz, Robert Grenier, Peter Quartermain, Jed Rasula, and Krzysztof Ziarek.

. . . sound . . . shape . . . meaning . . .

What is the shape of reading, the sound of a text as I read with the eye or the lips? How do I know the text—words on the page, words in the air? What is that arrangement of language on the two-dimensional page, the sculpture of sound in air? What is the meaning of sound in poetry? What is the relation between sound and meaning, sound and the visual shape of the poem on the page? How, in Zukofsky's

poetics—

$$\int_{\text{speech}}^{\text{music}}$$

An integral
Lower limit speech
Upper limit music

—is music the "upper limit" of writing, speech its "lower limit"?

Listening to Reading is about writing as an act of the mind playing with words across time and space that separates and connects them: the sound of words as memory (echo) of their physical shape, which is itself a memory (echo) of sound: the sound/shape of words and the world we know in words—words on the page (seen by the eye), words in the air (heard by the ear): dimension of letters on the page and in the air: weight of words as sound or silence waiting to become sound.

The essays that follow offer a critical and performative presentation of "experimental" writing—"avant-garde," "postmodern," "innovative," "language writing": I am less concerned with labels than with asking how this writing works, how it invites us to read—from Mallarmé, Stein, and Cage to books published in the '80s and '90s by Mei-mei Berssenbrugge, David Bromige, Clark Coolidge, Beverly Dahlen, Michael Davidson, Larry Eigner, Robert Grenier, Lyn Hejinian, Paul Hoover, Susan Howe, Ron Padgett, Michael Palmer, and Leslie Scalapino—writers whose work is viewed as difficult, ostensibly inaccessible, and has as yet been largely ignored by criticism.[1] My assumptions are (1) that the sound of a poem's words and their visual shape on the page are *interconnected:* that the sound of words is, literally, an acoustic shape (the shape of words in air), their shape literally a visual sound (letters waiting to become sound); (2) that meaning in poetry exists only in relation to sound (music/silence) and visual shape—that sound/shape articulates (and creates) meaning; (3) that the poem is less a representation/evidence/likeness of the world than its sound (echo), an event in which the world takes further shape; and (4) that the traditional border between criticism and/or theory and poetry is necessarily restrictive and may be usefully transcribed by a writing that "listens" to reading (i.e., that itself articulates/enacts the role that sound/shape plays in the composition, and also the perception, of poetry). In testing these premises, I will demonstrate and question how the poetries that are my subject might be read.

The book presents two different kinds of writing about poetry—critical analysis and performance—both of which pay particular attention to sound, shape, and the relation of sound/shape to meaning. The two kinds of writing alternate with each other (analysis, performance, analysis, performance, and so on) in order to suggest the "conversation" between them: readings whose purpose is to "explain" the writing that is their subject punctuated by "readings" whose purpose is to perform/demonstrate that writing by doing/enacting it. The reader will be able to experience, and distinguish between, these contrapuntal forms of writing: *analytic close reading* and *reading-as-writing-itself*—writing that in listening to reading engages its subject on, and in, its own terms.

"The Asymptote of Elsewhere," for example, which asks how writing and reading interact, lays out the ground upon which my reading/writing has been built; "Writing [Echoes] Writing" examines the intertextual nature of writing-as-memory/echo/quotation, writing that attempts to write the world but can't, and the strategies concomitant with that circumstance; and "Memo/ Re: Reading Stein" (on Stein's early works), "Writing/ Re: Memory" (on Lyn Hejinian) and "Listening to Reading" itself (on Leslie Scalapino) are critical/expository pieces in which I think about how to read Stein, Hejinian and Scalapino. Alternatively, "Con(   )Text" is an epigraph whose fifty parts "score" the white (silence/music) space of the empty, two-dimensional page with a series of "sound bytes" that will map the contextual landscape of the writing that is my subject; "Signature"—a poem/essay of memory, sound, echo, and counting—performs the writing I mean to explore; "Idea's Mirror" (on Susan Howe) and "Reading *Sun*" (on Michael Palmer)—whose two "voices," registered in roman and italics, interact and subordinate: reader interacting with writer, reading with writing; reader subordinate to writer, reading to writing, the roman voice (mine) to the italicized one (Howe or Palmer's)—are "close reading" for the initiate, writing that will demonstrate the intertextuality of writing itself; and "The Landscape (Body) of the Poem," a prose poem that is also criticism, closes my reading by returning to the sound of the world in words.

Inviting a full engagement from the reader even as it *itself* enacts such a response, the writing in these performative pieces challenges the reader to redefine his or her role (*as reader/listener*) in reading a text. It has permitted me "to say what I [have] to say," as John Cage puts it, "in a way that [will] exemplify it; that [will], conceivably, permit the listener to experience what I [have] to say rather than just hear about it."[2] It will also allow me to demonstrate correspondences between the poetries that are my subject and the sorts of critical claims—about writing, reading, and the alphabet—that might be made about such poetries; demonstrate how poetry and critical discourse interconnect, how writing *of* a given discourse is inextricably bound up with writing *in* a given discourse. Although admittedly difficult, this writing is also essential to the scheme of the book because it is an extension of the writing that is my subject: writing that is itself listening to reading.

Before I begin, some preliminary remarks about the relations between music (sound/silence), shape, meaning, and the written text in poetry. Sound in poetry may be thought of as dimension: the *acoustic* dimension, given that the text itself (letters spelled into words, "scored" with marks of punctuation) exists on the page in two *visual* dimensions—the horizontal axis of letters, syllables, words, spaces, the line; the vertical axis of a sequence of lines running down the page.[3] Whereas its sound (the sound of letters, syllables, words, lines) realizes, when the poem is read aloud (heard by reader/listener), a third dimension, which brings the two-dimensional text fully into the world: as articulated acoustic shape (sound-as-shape, the shape of the poem in the air/ear)—a shape that, until the poem on the page is read aloud, exists only in potential, as Olson suggests when he writes, "A poem is energy transferred from where the poet got it . . . by way of the poem itself to, all the way over to, the reader"[4] —reader who will, in hearing it, complete the circuit. Reading aloud, and listening to reading, is crucial to this realization.

Words read with the eye only, in private reading experience, register only part of the poem's reality/being (presence). Full presence, in the present, becomes realized only when *poem enters ear: through air, as words read aloud.* When we read the poem silently, with eyes (but not ears), we think semantic meaning is the key: "She sang beyond the genius of the sea." But to ask, What does Stevens mean here? is to miss the point; whereas, if we truly "listen" to reading we will experience the poem in its full three dimensions, as both visual text and sonic text, words on page *and* in air. So that we *hear* (here) four long *e* sounds ("She," "ge-" "-nius," "sea"), four *s* sounds ("She," "sang," "genius," "sea")—*hear* in other words the poem's articulation of acoustic shape—what the poet in writing *made* (shaped) on the page, going back to the root meaning of *poein,* to make, poet-as-maker.

Take the last line of Keats's "To Autumn" ("And gathering swallows twitter in the skies") for example—echoed at the end of Stevens's "Sunday Morning":

> And, in the isolation of the sky,
> At evening, casual flocks of pigeons make
> Ambiguous undulations as they sink,
> Downward to darkness, on extended wings

—sound in poem meaning to *enact* sound in world; beauty of world's sound (which poem "refers" to: *gathering swallows twitter in the skies*) registered (in words) as the sound the poet perceives in the world. Meaning can't be extracted (as "ideas") from the poem, as critics who write about poetry as if it were *only* (or simply) "ideas" tend to do[5] (I am thinking of the story about Degas, who said to his friend Valéry, "I am so full of ideas but can't write a poem!" to which Valéry replied, "But my dear Degas, poetry is made out of words, not ideas!"). Nor is the poem's meaning simply its "content" ("Content *never* equals meaning"[6]), its "knowledge" ("Knowledge is not *translated* into words when it is expressed. The words are not a translation of something else that was there before they were"[7]) or its "representation of the world" ("the essence of which Schönberg summed up in the statement that the painter paints a picture rather than what it represents"[8]). Rather, as meaning(s) in the world can be "read" from their sounds and shapes ("world as text," "life an open book"), the meaning of the poem *is* sound/shape—is known (seen/heard) as a complex of extended meaning ("signification" + sound + shape): *sound (shape) as thought,* to think in words being to think in shape and sound.

The sound/shape of words is not meaning, but *means*—what the ear hears (listening), eye sees (reading). As Vygotsky writes, "A word without meaning is an empty sound"[9]—an absence of acoustic shape. Shape as such (of letters, of words) being fully significant, the poem without sound makes no "sense" except as something other than what it is: letters on the page waiting to be read. Read aloud, words produce sound: sound a product of visual shape, which sound itself also produces. If one doesn't listen to reading, one can't hear what's going on in a poem's third dimension: if the tree falls in the forest (nobody around?), does it make a sound? Perhaps, or perhaps not, depending on the position of the perceiver, but given that the poem *is* made of words rather than ideas, concepts, knowledge, or representation of the world, those words—once they are read, at least—have/make sound of their own that *can* be heard, as Stein implies when she writes (on Matisse), "Some were listening again and again to this one telling about this one being one being in living."[10]

(Words printed on the page ["locked" in print] are like offstage actions an audience must imagine in a play: Ophelia's drowning in the stream, Hamlet's father's death-by-poison in the orchard—action we hear about in words but don't see performed physically on stage; actions that don't actually take place *in* the play except in the words used to "perform" them—words spoken by the actress playing Gertrude, actor playing the Ghost. Similarly, words *not* read aloud—not spoken—and so *not* heard, fail to deliver what's going on in the poem—or deliver, rather, *only* its physical shape on the page, and whatever substance, syntax, image, symbol might be drawn from that. Not in any case sound, the offstage *action* of sound which in a poem gets realized/enacted only when words enter the air/ear.)

The sound of words is a memory (echo) of their physical shape—shape of letters printed or drawn, of spaces between them; shape itself a memory (echo) of their sound (what is spoken sounds like "t-h-i-s"). What we notice in listening to reading is the actual, material "stuff" of language, which in fact we hardly notice at all, given that we tend to think the purpose of language is to "communicate." Hence the reason unnoticed effects are more effective, in poetry at least, than noticed ones: what we don't notice—the visual/acoustic shape of letters, spaces, words, lines—in reading or listening to reading is exactly what delivers the things we do—image, metaphor, symbol, and so on. Readers of the visual text, as well as listeners to the acoustic one, generally pay attention to the "message" (what the writer means to say), as if the sound and shape of the words themselves don't matter or count—which of course they do.

Let me spell out directly, then, the ground upon which the essays in *Listening to Reading* are built:

1. Listening to the rhythm/syntax of experience, the poet "hears" the world, which is transcribed in the words of the poem: "A sentence has been heard," as Stein writes, "[n]ow listen."[11]

2. In writing experience down (in words), the poet reaches out beyond herself toward an audience—the "addressee" of Kristeva's second dimension, those "strangers" to whom Stein refers when she says, "I write for myself and strangers"[12]—who in reading will see/hear the shape/sound of those words on the page, in the air.
3. The visual shape of the poem enacts—and is enacted by—its acoustic shape: the shape that fills the air/ear, once the poem is read aloud and heard, *as sound;* as Zukofsky writes, "In sincerity shapes appear concomitants of word combinations, precursors of (if there is continuance) completed sound."[13]
4. Made present by such enactment (perceived by the reader's eye as words-on-the-page, by the listener's ear as words-in-the-air), the poem's meaning does not exist separately from its visual/acoustic identity; to paraphrase Zukofsky, the visual/acoustic shape of the poem—on the page, in the air—is never apart from its meaning[14].
5. The reader/listener will, in that perception of the text, come to know and appreciate the aesthetic object, "there being some connection between liking and listening," as Stein says.[15]
6. Close reading of the text can lead to fuller understanding of how its words work to create meaning—how words echo the sound of the world; how, as Vygotsky puts it, "[b]ehind words . . . the independent grammar of thought, the syntax of word meaning"[16] registers the poet's experience of that world, reflects that world's syntax as the poet "reads" it.
7. "Listening to reading" gives *access* to that experience/meaning—of words *and* world—made present in the poem's words, as Heidegger suggests when he writes, "What is present comes to presence . . . along . . . lines of usage . . . enjoining and preserving . . . what is present"[17] (i.e., *in* words, as echo/enactment/memory *of* world, the relation between the *written text* [visual shape] and its *music* [sound/silence, shape-in-air] being the *site* of its meaning).

Exploring the ground of this poetics, the essays that follow will explore how the poetries that are my subject might as I say be read.

Con(   )Text

The way music speaks. Do not forget that a poem, even though it is composed in the language of information, is not used in the language-game of giving information.[1]

The fact that language as writing and language as speech are entirely separate is evident in the fact that they contribute to entirely separate sorts of work.[2]

Why imitate 'speech'? Various vehicle that American speech is in the different mouths of any of us, possessed of particular powers of colloquial usage, rhythmic pressure, etc., it is *only* such. *To me, all speeches say the same thing, or:* . . . I HATE SPEECH.[3]

Voice is a possibility for poetry not an essence.[4]

[A]ny new direction would require poets to look . . . at what a poem is actually made of—not images, not voice, not characters or plot, all of which appear on paper, or in one's mouth, only through the invocation of a specific medium, language itself.[5]

It is through language that we experience the world, indeed through language that meaning comes into the world and into being. . . . An analogous idea to that of language not accompanying but constituting the world is that language does not accompany "thinking."[6]

Like everything metaphysical the harmony between thought and reality is to be found in the grammar of the language.[7]

I want writing what *is* thought/ where *feeling* is/ *words are born.*[8]

I became more and more excited about how words which were the words that made whatever I looked at look like itself were not the words that had in them any quality of description.[9]

[W]hat interests me is the coincidence and juxtaposition of the words on the page in their natural formation (alphabetical order). In reference to each other, they have a story of their own.[10]

As soon as I start *listening* to the words, they reveal their own vectors and affinities, pull the poem into their own field of force, often in unforeseen directions, away from the semantic charge of the original impulse.[11]

The attention seems centered on linguistic details and the relations among *them,* rather than on what they might 'point to.'[12]

One is brought back to the entirety of the *single* word which is in itself a relation, an implied metaphor, an argument, a harmony or a dissonance.

The economy of presentation in writing is a reassertion of faith that the combined letters—the words—are absolute symbols for objects, states, acts, interrelations, thoughts about them. If not, why use words—new or old?[13]

[J]ust what are words & what do they do?[14]

—words are *words* (ancient 'horticultural' or 'hunting' magic or/ cultural habit persisting in some guise—much 'more' than we know)—the *world* is 'beyond us' yet given to the sentience, as something of language process is, each time—it's a 'speaking to the beyond' from the 'unknown depths of the soul' (or the unknown 'beyond' speaking to 'soul') that makes a commonplace articulated—two together ('nothing personal')—say what happens/ happening is said—[15]

The components of the poetic object continued: the sound and pitch emphasis of a word are never apart from its meaning.[16]

When I think in language there aren't "meanings" going through my mind in addition to the verbal expressions: the language itself is the vehicle of thought.[17]

A thought may be compared to a cloud shedding a shower of words. Precisely because thought does not have its automatic counterpart in words, the transition from thought to word leads through meaning.[18]

To be able to see and feel the force and weight of formations of words, dynamics that otherwise go unnoticed; to feel it as stuff, to sound the language, and in so doing to reveal its meanings.[19]

you want/ the fact/ of things/ in words,/ of words[20]

Words—consisting of syllables, in turn made up of *phones* that are denoted by letters that were once graphic symbols or pictures. Words grow out of affects of

A. Sight, touch, taste, smell
B. Hearing
C. Thought with respect to other words, the interplay of concepts.[21]

—think of *Keats* as really 'milking' words of all possible letter/ phonemic qualities without really challenging notion of English word/ morpheme as basic unit of 'meaning'—hence 'best effects' all-stress monosyllabic—"No, no, go not to Leth(e)"—"Where are the songs of Spring? Ay, where are they?"—because mind in work really does *want* to think phonemically, one sounds so 'dense & rich', tongued—slows down articulation so teeth, lips, whole vocal apparatus drawn in to pronouncing letters, reading it aloud—[22]

A poem : a context associated with 'musical' shape, musical with quotation marks since it is not of notes as music, but of words more variable than variables, and used outside as well as within the context with communicative reference.[23]

Often one word, phrase or sentence seems to follow another with little regard for the recognized imports of these signs and strings. Their concatenation seems governed not by their referents, or by relations among them, but by features and relations intrinsic to them as language objects.[24]

Not "death" of the referent—rather a recharged use of the multivalent referential vectors that any word has, how words in combination tone and modify the associations made for each of them, how 'reference' then is not a one-on-one relation to an 'object' but a perceptual dimension that closes in to pinpoint, nail down (*this* word), sputters omnitropically (the in in the which of who where what wells), refuses the build up of image track/ projection while, pointillistically, fixing a reference at each turn . . .[25]

In other words, poems are not referential, or at least not importantly so.[26]

Referentiality is diminished by organizing the language around other features or axes, around features which make present to us words' lack of transparency, their physicality, their refusal to be motivated along schematic lines by frames exterior to themselves. Refusing to 'point,' or to be arranged according to a 'pointing system,' they risk the charge of being pointless. That is, to be a self-sufficiency of event—confounding the inadequation of words and referents that we mistakenly call meaning. This is not meaning. Instead, this is meaning. *This.*[27]

This is how we think. *This* is how we act. *This* is how we talk about it.[28]

Talk about poetry has at some point got to be abstract, in order to maintain itself in relation to the poetry.[29]

One would like to speak of the *function* of the word, of what it does, in this sentence. As of the function of a lever in a machine. But what does this function consist in? How does it come to light? For there isn't anything hidden, is there? We see the whole sentence all right. The function must reveal itself in the course of the calculus.[30]

[T]he desire is to reveal the specificity, the tone and texture as much as 'content' 'summary' (of experience). Making writing, the activity itself, an active process, the fact of its own activity, autonomous, self-sufficient.[31]

[I]n the early 70s, when John Cage used chance operations to compose a long four-part poem made up of language elements drawn from H.D. Thoreau's *Journals,* he called it *Empty Words,* implying that these words, etc., have no "content."[32]

it's very tiny, content[33]

[W]ords can be brought into one's more total awareness in reading, where in reading you are brought up short to the point of the text becoming viscerally present to you, the 'content' and the 'experience of reading' are collapsed onto each other, the content being the experience of reading, the consciousness of the language and its movement and sound, the page.[34]

Writing is reading. I live in a world of signs which acausally direct my consciousness. . . . At the root of all comprehension exists an indeterminate number of possible meanings which are coming into being, into consciousness.[35]

Consciousness is reflected in a word as the sun in a drop of water. A word relates to consciousness as a living cell relates to a whole organism, as an atom relates to the universe. A word is a microcosm of human consciousness.[36]

The conception of a text as a map or model whose final constitution requires the reader's active response is a theory of reading.[37]

Texts read the reader.

. . . .

Readers embody texts.
Physical language.[38]

Distance, rather than absorption, is the intended effect.[39]

The images do not reflect back. They are only themselves, which is not in relation to existence.[40]

"Along the coast, on cots, in coats. A warm new storm. Blue ink on a white page between red lines." This is not a diarist's record of observed detail; no eye ("I") could be this ubiquitous. It is the realism of language, language under pressure, fully present.[41]

[A] poetry of visible borders: a poetry of shape . . . emphasizes its medium as being constructed, rule governed, everywhere circumscribed by grammar & syntax, chosen vocabulary: designed, manipulated, picked, programmed, organized, & so an artifice, artifactual—monadic, solipsistic, homemade, manufactured, mechanized & formulaic at some points: willful.[42]

I am in a dialogue when I write a poem, but not with a prospective reader, not even the "ideal reader," but with language itself.[43]

The terms Coolidge uses in talking about Eigner are the terms language would use in talking about itself:

> an invisible & steadying "is" behind everything . . . all particles in the pile soon to reach/ *nounal state* . . . the word "air" & its immediate prepositioning . . . these "scenes" don't exist, never have . . . the poem is built// each line/ equals/ its own completion// and every next line/ its consequence . . . wholes are made only by motion . . . Each poem sights into a distance of all the others following . . . word-activation of the imagination in the act of seeing . . . a synthesis of presence.

Here "the self" has become generalized as "language," or, put another way, "the self" has exploded and disappeared.[44]

Rather than making the language as transparent as possible . . . (by creating, stylistically, the illusion of the invisibility of wordness and structure), the movement is toward opacity/denseness—visibility of language through the making translucent of the medium. To actually map the fullness of thought and its movement. Cut of mind/ perception/grain of mind . . . to . . . the factness of the world in the factness of the poem. Poem becoming a perceptual field/ experience 'independent' of 'author'.[45]

The weight of the writing at the tip of the hand/ just as it enters the paper . . .[46]

The phrases' meaning/reading isn't other than their entwined imposition in being drawn.[47]

Language is no longer an intermediary between the writer and the world or between the concept of the work and content. Language is not the instrument of expression but the substance. It is inseparable from the world, since it is in the nature of language to be entangled in a system of reference and cross-reference.[48]

So to go from 'thinking' as an activity of 'self' to a world creating/perceiving idea. *Thinking things the world.* So that in the end the poem stands as another particular being, hence object, like myself, in the world, and I beside it.[49]

> The book will, therefore, draw a limit to thinking, or rather—not to thinking, but to the expression of thoughts; for, in order to draw a limit to thinking we should have to be able to think both sides of this limit (we should therefore have to be able to think what cannot be thought).[50]

The Asymptote of Elsewhere

> How much what is sounded by words has to do with what is seen by them—and how much what is both sounded and seen by them crosscuts an interplay among themselves—will naturally sustain the scientific definition of poetry we are looking for. To endure it would be compelled to integrate these functions: time, and what is seen in time (as held by a song), and an action whose words are actors or, if you will, mimes composing steps as of a dance that at proper instants calls in the vocal chords to transform it into plain speech.
>
> —Louis Zukofsky, "Poetry"

Poetry from the time of Plato (who banished poets from his republic for telling "lies" about the real world) has generally been understood to stand in opposition to philosophy and science, both of which aim to discover the truth of that world, whatever that may be. This opposition—between fact and fiction, methodology and imagination—assumes that the world we live in can be known and understood in one of two mutually exclusive ways: first as a system of coherences whose physics may be described objectively in language (words, numbers, symbols, formulae); second as the raw material, the natural resources, from which a coherent system—subjectively coherent, also in language—might be made: "sounding the words to see what they tell, to make their resonances tangible, and, specifically, with the realization that we literally make the world come into being by giving voice to it, by our (re)calls. (*words, words/ as if all/ worlds were there*—Robert Creeley, 'A Token'.)"[1]

Calling into question the ancient schism between poetry and science and philosophy is the notion, passed down from Plotinus through Blake and Shelley to Yeats and, among others in our own time, Duncan and Spicer, that poetry as a gift from the Muse provides access to absolute truth, through divine inspiration and revelation, the poet acting as conduit through which outside forces speak. According to this theory, the operation of external forces, which themselves order the world that science attempts to explain, is dictated *through* the divinely inspired poet, thus making poetry itself a science. The poet in this case works not for him- or herself but as a medium or secretary in the service of a master, the God behind the world's veil. The poet "hears" this God, perhaps, as Yeats describes it, by falling into a trancelike state of semiconsciousness: "we are lured to the threshold of sleep, and it may be far beyond it, without knowing that we have ever set our feet upon the steps of horn or ivory."[2] As Nietzsche put it, "Provided one has the slightest remnant of superstition left, one can hardly reject completely the idea that one is the mere incarnation, or mouthpiece, or medium of some almighty power."[3] Taking "superstition" not pejoratively but in its root sense (to stand above, beyond), this looks back at least as far as Plato in the *Ion,* who seems himself to admit some place for the poet: "The God would show us, lest we doubt, that these lovely poems are not of man or human workmanship, but are divine and from the gods, and that the poets are nothing but interpreters of the gods, each one possessed by the divinity to whom he is in bondage."[4] Instead of imagining subjectively, that is, or making up fictions only representative of fact, the inspired poet articulates *what is,* sinks into the belly of the world of words to discover there not simply that the rose is a *rosa spinosissima* (or Scotch Rose) but that "A rose is a rose is a rose is a rose."

Stein's paratactic "nonsense" here—*not* nonsense since these words may be (or make) an equivalent of "a rose," as she herself claims when she says that the rose appears here for the first time in over 200 years of English poetry—may suggest how the words of poetry connect with, and can be made an object of, the work of empirical science. Consider *Tender Buttons,* written in what seems to have been, judging from Mable Dodge's eye-witness account of her writing habits at the Villa Curonia in 1912, a series of trancelike states similar to the one Yeats ascribes to the inspired poet:

> Gertrude always worked at night. After everyone was asleep she used to sit . . . writing automatically in a long weak handwriting—4 or 5 lines to the page—letting it ooze up from deep inside her, down on to the paper with the least possible physical effort; she would cover a few pages so and leave them there and go to bed, and in the morning Alice would gather them up the first thing and take them off and type them. Then she and Gertrude would always be so surprised and delighted at what she had written, for it had been done so unconsciously she'd have no idea what she'd said the night before.[5]

Such an activity of mental operation produced for Stein paragraphs like these from the end of "Orange In," which Herbert Marks calls a modern instance of that "prophetic stammer—the 'slow tongue' of Moses and its variations, the 'unclean lips of Isiah,' the demur of Jeremiah, the mutism of Ezekiel," which corresponds to "the moment of blockage that marks the mind's defeat before the unattainability of the object. It symbolizes not the transcendent order but the prophet's relation to the transcendent order, a relation that includes his mute intuition of his own infinitude"[6]:

> Pain soup, suppose it is a question, suppose it is butter, real is, real is only, only excreate, only excreate a no since.
>
> A no, a no since, a no since when, a no since when since, a no since when since a no since when since, a no since, a no since when since, a no since, a no, a no since a no since, a no since, a no since.[7]

How we take this depends on how far we are willing to allow the sinews of ordinary languge to be stretched. The attentive reader will I think hear Stein step ("stammering" to say what must be said) across the line that divides (apparent) sense from (only apparent) nonsense: will hear the deliberate accretion of monosyllables divided in the last paragraph by commas into increasingly larger syntactic units—two words, three words, four words, five words, and so on—which themselves seem to go nowhere, as we expect words in recognizable semantic contexts should, simply in that these words begin to double back and repeat themselves again and again in the same recurrent patterns, almost like a code built of four terms—*a, no, since,* and *when*—into a forty-nine-word "message," which only the most persistent, or playful, of readers will think to decode. To that reader, I should think, the formula *a no since* said fast often enough sounds inevitably like *innocence,* which, followed five times as it is here by *when*—"innocence when"—sets up unseen but heard lines of connection, what Marks calls "the insistence of semantic phantoms, which gather about every rhythmically or phonetically modulated text like dead souls about a sacrifice,"[8] back through the poem to its title, "Orange In" (read "origin," a poem concerned to map the structure of the moment thought begins).

What does this passage from Stein have to do with science, taken generally, and what it does vis-à-vis the world it means to decipher? By which I mean to ask, how is Stein's act of composition, in writing the words *a, no, since,* and *when* in sequence one after another through the lines of this paragraph, like the research of a biologist such as Bruce Pavlik, who studies how the ecosystem of the Eureka Valley—a desolate stretch of windblown sand nestled below the fourteen-thousand-foot peaks of the White Mountains on the far eastern border of California, which supports a species of grass left over from prehistory and found nowhere else on earth; or the research of a biochemist such as Tom White, whose work at the University of California in Berkeley may lead to a cure for AIDS; or the research of a theoritical physicist (name withheld) who attempts to explain the behavior of matter so small no one has ever observed it? By which I mean also to ask, how do the forms of emotion and feeling that have since the Greeks been viewed as the province of poetry—Stein herself calls them to our attention in her famous discovery, first made while listening to her dog Basket drinking, about the difference between sentences and paragraphs: "Sentences are not emotional but paragraphs are"—connect to the world of the biologist or physicist; just as, conversely, what part does reason and thought play in the work of the poet, especially the poet who writes "Orange In"?

Attempting to locate the terms of an answer to such questions, think of Pound circa 1934, whose *ABC of Reading* posits a ground upon which the ancient quarrel between poetry and science can be resolved: "The proper METHOD for studying poetry and good letters is the method of contemporary biologists, that is careful first-hand examination of the matter, and continual COMPARISON of one 'slide' or specimen with another."[9] Which is simply to say that one reads the poem *closely,* with the same act of attention—focused at both micro- and wide-angle range—to the surface, tilt, and interior thrust of a particular structure in words that the scientist brings to his study of observable (or supposed) phenomena. Pound's anecdote of the French biologist Louis Agassiz and the fish is worth remembering (for "fish" here read "text"):

> A post-graduate student equipped with honours and diplomas went to Agassiz to receive the final and finishing touches. The great man offered him a small fish and told him to describe it.

> Post-Graduate Student: 'That's only a sunfish.'
>
> Agassiz: 'I know that. Write a description of it.'
>
> After a few minutes the student returned with the description of the Ichthus Heliodiplodokus or whatever term is used to conceal the common sunfish from vulgar knowledge, family of Heliichtherinkus, etc., as found in textbooks of the subject.
>
> Agassiz again told the student to describe the fish.
>
> The student produced a four-page essay. Agassiz then told him to look at the fish. At the end of three weeks the fish was in an advanced state of decomposition, but the student knew something about it.[10]

Again I say for "fish" read "text," about which the reader will know "something" beyond the self-reflexive generalities by which criticism becomes a hall of mirrors; "something" beyond "Icthus Heliodiplodokus," that is, "something" about the words on the page and, when read aloud, in the air. (To read "text" for "fish," I should add, alters Pound's use of this anecdote, since Pound meant to suggest that words could, through attention to *other* phenomena, be brought closer to things, *not* that words and verbal procedures could themselves be taken as "objects" of investigation; Pound was blind to Stein.) Nor does the connection between scientific and poetic method end here, since the poet must also (and first) arrange particular words in a particular order, the physics of which convention and history determine to be meaningful (i.e., valuable, therefore memorable).

The point is *attention*—the *attention* one gives to concrete "events" in words as well as the world; as Pound, who had a rather simplistic notion of the immediate relation between words and things, writes (quoting a French commentator on Einstein), "Science does not consist in inventing a number of more or less abstract entities corresponding to the number of things you wish to find out."[11] Rather, assuming that theory is *only* theory (not to be confused with "facts"), empirical science examines observable phenomena in the world, knowledge of which, arrived at through precise attention to detail, is made present in the language of science: quantitative description, formulae, symbols, graphs, and so on. Likewise for the poet, whose aim is not to translate feeling, thought, and perception about the world into words but rather to create, enact, sound, and echo (literally "re-member") that world in words, making it present in a world that language itself makes real—a world in which words are what most count.

The intersection between the methods of poetry and science—what the poet (or reader) does in writing (or reading), what the scientist does in discovering and describing the world—may be seen in the work of Andreas Vesalius, whose dissections of human and animal cadavers before hundreds of spectators crammed into the temporary and later permanent anatomy "theaters" of Padua and Bologna, and documented in a six-hundred-plus-page illustrated volume entitled *De humani corporis fabrica libri septum* (now known universally as the *Fabrica*) published in Basel in 1543, marks what Glenn Harcourt in a recent essay on Vesalius calls "the constitution of anatomy as a modern descriptive science."[12] Harcourt discusses the text and illustrations of the *Fabrica* in terms of the synthesis of Renaissance art and science, seeing it as "work in which a comprehensive and explicitly scientific program articulated through a complex interaction of descriptive text and descriptive image becomes an essentially artistic artifact"—i.e., an evident construct, "the fact/ of things/ in words,/ of words." Vesalius's illustrations present visceral anatomy "as if through the dissection of fragmentary antique sculpture," standing in marked contrast to modern textbook photographs of dissected viscera so tightly framed and focused "as to become both visually and conceptually dissociated from the physical body whose dissection it so artlessly transcribes." Harcourt's essay includes both the modern photograph whose pared-down caption reads: "Abdominal cavity. Mesenterium. The small intestine has been laterally reflected to demonstrate the mesentery"; and a sixteenth-century draftsman's rendering of a dissection performed by Vesalius, whose substantively comparable but longer-winded caption acknowledges both his physical act of dissection and its record by the draughtsman:

> In [this figure] the peritoneum has been dissected away, the omentum removed, and we have also fractured some ribs so that the entire hollow of the liver could be drawn more conveniently. Then the orifices of the stomach are seen since it, as well as the intestine, have been pushed to the left in order to bring into view the whole of the mesentery.[13]

But however much Vesalius may have brought art to bear upon science, his work in person and as recorded in the *Fabrica* presents, as he describes it, "in sufficient detail the number, site, shape, size, substance, connection to other parts, use and function of each part of the human body,"—an account that suggests how one might think to read, in order to understand, not only the body as a text, as Vesalius did and as modern physicians continue to do, but the text as a body whose details—number, shape, substance, connection to other parts, function, and so on—are equally subject to sharp, precise, surgically exact scrutiny by both the poet (who writes it) and the reader (who reads).

In closing, I will return to Zukofsky, who writes, "In poems, as in works of science, the involved susceptibilities always function with respect to some concept of exactness of utterance."[14] Those "susceptibilities" involve language, which as Charles Bernstein says,

> is the material of both thinking and writing. We think and write in language, which sets up an intrinsic connection between the two.
>
> Just as language is not something that is separable from the world, but rather is the means by which the world is constituted, so thinking cannot be said to 'accompany' the experiencing of the world in that it informs that experiencing. It is through language that we experience the world, indeed through language that meaning comes into the world and into being. As persons, we are born into language and world; they exist before us and after us. Our learning language is learning the terms by which a world gets seen.[15]

To learn those terms is, for poet and scientist alike, an essential act; as Zukofsky elsewhere writes, "[t]he poet, no less than the scientist, works on the assumption that inert and live things and relations hold enough interest to keep him alive as part of nature. The fact that he persists with them confirms him."[16] So too for the attentive reader, who like the poet/scientist approaching words and world with precision reads the sound of thought as the language it finds to trace itself; who also like the poet, as Zukofsky writes, "measure[s] by means of words, whose effect as offshoot of nature may (or should) be that their strength of suggestion can never be accounted for completely"; who finally might take as a model Paul Valéry, here described by physicist Louis de Broglie in his preface to Valéry's *Cahiers:*

> What actually complemented in a unique manner Paul Valéry's qualities of imagination and poetic sensibility was a great love of general ideas, a constant tendency towards precision in images and terms, a *finesse d'esprit* at times reaching subtlety. Thus, he could find in the development of modern science all that suited his mind: the clarity of concepts and words, the suddenly discovered vast intellectual horizons, the fine subtlety of theories which, revealing lapses of logic, unforeseen properties of forms and numbers, the relativity of time and space and the uncertainties of the atomic world, have opened for human thought strange new perspectives. And Paul Valéry, poet with a penetrating insight, knew how to envision, behind the dryness of experimental facts and the coldness of logorithms and theories, this triumphant conquest of the unknown, this ascendant march toward the splendor of the True, which constitutes the value and the poetry of Science.[17]

[Echoes]

What happens when words approach the conditon of music? In what sense *is* music the "upper limit" of speech? How *does* the sound of words echo (and also, if noticed, "influence") their shape and meaning—world's sound and shape and meaning? What *is* the relation between words and their sounds, sounds and their shapes on the page and in the air, sounds and shapes and meaning?

Consider Thomas Morley, whose setting of these words to music changes them (and us):

> No, no, Nigella!
> Let who list prove thee
> I cannot love thee.
> Have I deserved
> Thus to be served?
> Well then content thee,
> If thou repent thee.
> —*The First Booke of Balletts to Five Voyces* (1595)

We hear five voices, intoning a "no" that becomes in effect negative to the fifth power—soprano, high D; second soprano, B; alto or tenor, G; tenor or bass, D; bass, G below C; followed by three more intonations of that same "no" in each part; multiplied by five parts, equals twenty times "no" in a fabric of sound so insistent how could Nigella, whoever she may be, think the answer (to what question?) might be other than "no":

Figure 1 Thomas Morley, from *The First Booke of Balletts to Five Voyces* (1595)

After the third verse line, "I cannot love thee" (rejection, farewell, the breaking off of love conventional though it may be) a listener ("Nigella," say, or anyone who can empathize) will hear:

Figure 2 Thomas Morley, from *The First Booke of Balletts to Five Voyces* (1595)

A second barrage of apparently meaningless syllables enters at the end of the first stanza, when the words hold out their sudden hope of happiness in love "If thou repent thee," after which the nonsense of fa la las speeding as much as eight or sixteen times *faster* than the words just sung, the map of music making of words a grid whose staggered starts and stops overlap in sheets too dense to be unfolded by ear alone, though eye can discern from score what goes on at any given point.

---

triads, the same kind
involving
consecutive fifths

"If the singing of words is to be thought of as intoned speech, which it is, then for any singer the main question is: 'Who's talking?'" (Virgil Thomson).[1] One thinks of improvisation, then, not by the poet or composer but by the speaker, as in *Semper Dowland, Semper Dolens:* that repeats may be heard filling the viola part with notes rising and slowly falling to a final touch at the root of what begins in the next bar, say measure, as music times thought's next step.

---

what the words note, short
of meaning
pace say, legs that stride

What happens when the words of a poem are put into the air by a voice or voices intoning syllables at certain precisely measured pitches held for certain precisely indicated durations? And how is it that when the words of a poem are sung the result in its effect is *more* than either of its constituent components, its words, its music? The quality of feeling (if it can be called that provisionally) sail forward, as if to register the singer/speaker's heart's core, as in Dowland's air "Flow My Tears."

---

the page opposite
songs, of which
the highest "compasse"

Four of the five voice parts of Gesualdo's "Io parto" (1611):

Second Soprano	Io parto e non piu dissi
Tenor	Io parto e non piu dissi
Alto	Io parto e non piu dissi
Bass	Io parto e non piu dissi

begin declamatorily, all four voices singing at once with words clear into air, everything that follows straining emotion as words fracture, bend, twist, half- and quarter-turns that aim to explore what range of emotion and sense it might be possible to arrive at, singing.

---

how long a silence
before this
of faces, bodies

Morley tells us that after dinner, "music books (according to custom) being brought to the table, the mistress of the house presented me with a part earnestly requiring me to sing":[2]

Soprano	April is in my Mistress' face,	April is
Alto	April is in my Mistress' face	
Tenor		April is
Bass		April is

After this relatively straightforward beginning of parts (Soprano singing with Alto, Tenor with Bass) the identities of separate voices begin to collapse, convolute:

Soprano	in my Mistress' face my Mistress; face, April is			
Alto	April is in my Mistress'face			April is
Tenor	in my Mistress'	face,	April is in my Mistress'	
Bass	in my Mistress' face		April is in my Mistress'	

---

the sort of performance
one *is,* one
stamped the other hand

Another kind of repetition: when voices sing the same or different syllables in unison one hears vertical as well as linear sound, the words on top of one another high to low, soprano-alto-tenor-bass. ("When you see this sign :||: of repetition you must begin again, making the notes next before the sign (be it minim, crotchet, or whatsoever) a semibreve in the first singing." [Morley, 99])

At this repeat, both
Altus and
Quintus exchange parts

Measured song, a property of singing, is nothing else but the difference between thought and the sound it makes, thinking pitch. What one poet would make of his perception the moment brain synapse fires, chemistry of cells, pink light on the wall the morning calls, the world already well awake.

---

pronounced—really pronounced
in proportion to
one such matter, creatures

Music delivers the emotional impact of the text, as if the single word could come forward or lift above its role in the text of all words, whose background the key determines will be spent, making that once the feeling most concerned.

---

after a list called
days, a base
two or three say, more

"And therefore those plainsongs which were so contained were called 'natural' because every key of their six notes stood invariable the one to the other however the notes were named, as from D sol re to E la mi always a whole note whether one did sing sol la or Re mi, and so forth of others" (Morley, 111)

---

if ground on a page
wants comfort
conscious—continuous

Marenzio's "Solo e pensoso i più deserti campi" (1500), the voice taking notes or measure of when the syllables should be spoken/sung, express all that (dis)content could mean. Petrarch's text, which would have us believe the fiction of sole self, "alone and pensive, the deserted fields/ I measure with deliberate and slow steps," pulling at the edges of one's ability to follow such a falling forward. Or trying to be able to stop.

---

to be written about
under feet
as find "things" to do

Gesualdo, the most experimental of all the Italians, looking to the color of chromaticism as clear message of the text, because everything that unfolds say from the opening line—"*Io parto e non più dissi che il dolore*"—aims to hear the words, their pull to the heart of what meaning can approach in the body of the person who hears and so *does* feel their pull. The pluck of a stringed instrument circa 1600 is no different today, can't it be said, in the condition we face knowing the truth the words are sign to. Everything that unfolds is an emotional response to the *what* of the line, its play to sympathy or content, what in the medium of language could rhyme with (echo) the world sense perceives, say of the body as it leaves the room, closing the glass door.

---

the air one thinks is
thick, staircase
like a letter, tree

Or take the freedom to break a text, emphasize the motion and emotion of syllables each of *whom* carry the sign of what's missing, wanted, or found. "—not being careful to see the strokes meet just at right angles . . . this figure, '♮' . . . confounded with the sign . . . which is this, '𝄪' . . . made thus, 'X'" (Morley, 110).

Expressionism
lying down
oxygen, leaves the bells

So that one can hear each note clearly, the better and more attractive the embellishment that lifts or drags syllables where without notes no sense of that would be, say on *fained, pit-, at, long, -nough, place, joyes, cold, freeze.*

---

ascending a third,
descending,
ascending a fourth

This too is a kind of improvisation. The singer sings it in a way another would not think of, but would herself sing with *other* notes, each configuration (of notes) having its own name and *meaning,* if that could be said with respect to pitch on a fixed scale.

Pavana Lachrimae:
John Dowland
sett foorth by Wm. Byrd

Or what is it that happens when one hears several voices intoning different words or parts of words at once? The same instance say to sound *tears, like, like, to, the, mor-, the, mor-, -ning, -ning,* then, at once, *showers*—as if that sudden resolution to the problem of how to get things said by most direct means, the economics of the syllable as currency in a system whose standard of exchange is the language it lifts by increments into the air.

---

back up stairs, descending
starter kind
of meaning a voice

The sense music delivers of space, as in air the notes could fill were they sent full blown (voiced or plucked) outward, the body then entering that space *between* one who sings and one who listens, not the reader (merely) but now active participant, co-conspirator in the creation of what comes to be known (through the ear) as meaning, the feeling of it *who living had no note.*

---

horizon ochre
painting, drift
can be something one sees

The rhythm of the galliard, say, as one-two-three-four followed by lift the dancer would raise a foot or hand to partner, the other half to whom words "Awake, sweet love" have been addressed as premonitory to love, the act of which song stands as foreplay. (One hears the soprano on top of other voices, leading the way, the pairing of other dance steps inside the circle written out as notes the lute plays, up to and including repeats.)

---

hear the door, a shirt
someone wears
to think the sense of

The intervals of two falling fourths in Dowland's "Flow, my tears, fall from your springs" want resolution. In the performance of such a thought sung to notes whose impulse is to move (down or up) to where the pitch can *stay* closed, notes as echo stopped, one hears the poet's "voice" in a musical dimension whose boundaries are defined in range by pitches the voice sings (strings following) as layers in the fabric of sound whose threads weave the texture of feeling the words would at best suggest. So that what the reader of words alone can at most *imagine,* the emotion say behind these lines,

Flow, my tears, fall from your springs!
Exiled for ever let me mourn;
Where night's black bird her sad infamy sings,
There let me live forlorn

becomes known by the addition that is the expansion of *sound* ordered by these "directions" of notes—how the words will be delivered—not then through eye (the reader's) to brain but ear (the listener's) as port to what sense most means, unfolding sound:

Figure 3 John Dowland, from *The Second Booke of Songs or Ayres* (1600)

this is a song for
calling back
spirits of the dead

The feeling "behind" or "of" these words, say of a person being "sad" or "depressed," the music brings out as pure *emotion,* so that when one hears the song being sung by this voice, accompanied by lute and bass, one is taken farther (emotionally) than by the words by themselves, to where meaning becomes visceral, stunning. The music makes adjustment to our perception of text, what we think we hear when we read those words.

say "in the hills of Thailand"
gymnastics
the air, local, shapes

In Morley's anthology *The Triumphes of Oriana* (1601), composed of madrigals he collected from twenty-three of his contemporaries, each song ends with the words "Long live fair Oriana." When Thomas Weelkes set that line to six voice parts, he pulled out all the stops so to speak, in order to play at what words set to music might make as fabric/sheets of sound:

Figure 4 Thomas Weelkes, from *The Triumphes of Oriana to* 5 *and* 6 *Voyces* (1601)

---

what part of you is
the poem, lute
the sound of wings and beaks

The twentieth song in Morley's *Canzonets. Or Little Short Songs to Three Voyces* (1593), "Arise, get up, my dear," is a kind of mini-Epithalamium calling for the bride to wake and prepare herself for the rites of marriage. But the music to which these words are sung makes such "reading" beside the point, in that a listener can all but *not hear* the words, nor discern their "sense," music in effect overwhelming the meaning of the words—words set to music having become fractured, fragmented, broken apart, broken down say into the syllable-as-unit-of-(non)sense. For example, when this portion of the line "Spice cakes, sops in wine are now a dealing" is sung, one is likely to hear different particles sung at the same time: "sops" plus "wine" plus "are," "in" plus "O" plus "a," "wine" plus "fine" plus "deal-." The song in effect moves at each point both horizontally, along the line, and vertically, as stacks of syllables that, sounded simultaneously, create meanings more complex than those made when the line is "read" by a single voice:

Soprano: deal - ing spice cake sops in wine
Alto: spice cake sops in wine, O fine, spice cake sops in
Tenor: spice cake sops in wine, sops in wine

Soprano: sops in wine are now a deal - ing
Alto: wine, O fine, are a deal - ing
Tenor: are a deal - ing, are a - deal - ing

---

across the table
voices round
a corner, swerving

Look at how the setting of these last lines of the poem generates the confusion of frenetic action the words "talk about" but, by themselves, leave to a reader's imagination—action the same words sung to notes put into the air, as real as event itself:

Soprano: and how the maids jerk it, with Kate and Will
Alto: and see how the maids jerk it, jerk it,
Tenor: how the maids jerk it, with Kate and Will, Tom and Jill

Soprano: Tom and Jill, now a skip, then a trip fine-ly set a
Alto: with Kate and Will, and Jill, now a trip, then a skip,
Tenor: hey ho brave, now a skip, then a trip, fine - ly

Soprano: -loft there a-gain as oft hey ho bless - ed
Alto: fine-ly set a - loft, there a-gain as oft O fine
Tenor: set a loft all for fair Daph - ne's Daph ne's

Soprano: ho - li - ho - li - day.
Alto: brave ho - - - li - day.
Tenor: wed - ding wed - ding day.

---

the car whose brakes squeal
as it angles
left (miraculous)

Or to see/hear the violence music might wreak upon the words of a text, think of the fifth song in Morley's *The First Book of Canzonets To Two Voyces* (1595):

> Miraculous, love's wounding!
> E'en those darts my sweet Phyllis
> So fiercely shot against my heart rebounding,
> Are turned to roses, violets and lilies,
> With odor sweet abounding.

One composition in music fractures a second attendant composition in words. The result is a staggering of voices, like starting a race around a track, the person in the outside lane going first, leading off, followed by others who catch and then pass him, perhaps, only to be overtaken toward the end, a photo finish. Here say the words of the soprano and tenor parts printed out as separate strands, linear but circular, the same words repeating (hypnotically) again and again:

> *Soprano:* Miraculous love's wounding, love's wounding, miraculous love's wounding, miraculous love's wounding. Miraculous love's wounding, miraculous love's wounding, miraculous love's wounding. E'en those darts my sweet Phyllis, E'en those darts my sweet Phyllis, So fiercely shot against my heart rebounding, rebounding. Are turn'd to roses, violets and lilies, violets and lilies, with odor sweet abounding sweet abounding, with odor sweet abounding. Miraculous love's wounding, miraculous love's wounding, miraculous love's wounding, miraculous love's wounding, love's wounding, miraculous love's wounding, miraculous love's wounding.

Tenor: Miraculous love's wounding, miraculous love's wounding, miraculous love's wounding. Miraculous love's wounding, love's wounding, miraculous love's wounding, miraculous love's wounding. E'en those darts my sweet Phyllis, E'en those darts my sweet Phyllis, so fiercely shot against my heart rebounding, rebounding, rebounding. Are turn'd to roses, violets and lilies, violets and lilies, with odor sweet abounding, with odor sweet abounding. Miraculous love's wounding, love's wounding, miraculous love's wounding, miraculous love's wounding. Miraculous love's wounding, miraculous love's wounding, miraculous love's wounding.

---

blasting words a part
music calls
what it means to speak

Words register an emotion, sadness say, or excitement: he's "up" or "down." And music, assuming it "follows" words in the order or process of composition (which might assume as well a simultaneity of that process, putting words and music forward together as collaboration in the trading of "parts" or "voices" as in improvisatory jazz, a conversing then of the two mediums), plays into that emotion, pushes it toward what amounts to emotion "squared," that quality of feeling to which words as abstract sign refer (that is to say, *point*).

---

the voice about to
enter air
which came first, of course

Think of music as the echo of thought, as in Campion's poem "Follow Your Saint," whose words ask that its music follow a person as echo—"the music that her echo is"—a person who in the convention isn't so much a unique individual as "she" is one's "thought": who or what such a person might be. As if music were the echo of a person who is herself an idea and so might be *the echo of thought* (and words): how the words of poems set to music are echoed by that music, when the voice that sings the words puts them into the air.

---

common daylight, think
the beat is
as words hit, accent

Music can slow the words down, so that when one reads the words to the first stanza of this poem:

> Follow your saint, follow with accent sweet,
> Haste you, sad notes, fall at her flying feet.
> There, wrapped in cloud of sorrow, pity move,
> And tell the ravisher of my soul I perish for her love:
> But, if she scorns my never-ceasing pain,
> Then burst with sighing in her sight and ne'er return again.

the tempo at which one reads it "normally" is faster than what one hears in a performance of the song. Notes can also pick up the length of syllables and make them more definite:

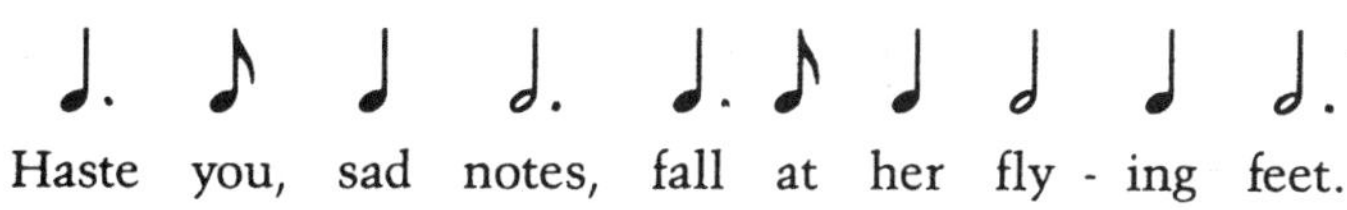

Figure 5 Thomas Campion, from *A Book of Ayres* (1601)

But in a line like "And tell the ravisher of my soul I perish for her love," the quick little words ("And," "the," "of," "my," "I," "for," "her") and syllables ("rav-ish-er") that one would tend to read relatively quickly are instead slowed by the music, which *drags* them as if across the rocks of this speaker's exposed, heart-felt concern.

> rhythm as form, tea
> when it leaves
> the cup a white ridge

Music is there to *serve* the words, as speaker is there to serve the lady. It follows the words the way music is supposed to follow the person who is herself *made of words* (thought). So to ask, Are words in the foreground, notes meant to set them forward, as into ear?

> an arrangement, cord
> mandate or
> date with man whose hand

Or think of the difference between the words of this poem:

> In darkness let me dwell, the ground shall sorrow be;
> The roof despair to bar all cheerful light from me;
> The walls of marble black that moistened still shall weep;
> My music hellish jarring sounds to banish friendly sleep.
> Thus wedded to my woes, and bedded to my tomb,
> O let me living, living die, till death do come.

and these same words sung to John Dowland's music. Pace for one thing: it must take five times as long to sing the song (with duration of notes, musically dictated repeats, rests, and so on) as it does to read its words only. This is now a performance—by musician and singer who projects words into the air accompanied by notes that sometimes dictate they slow down or speed up or go up or go down in pitch, and sometimes *repeat* in ways the words by themselves do not. Look at what happens to the words of the poem's last line ("O let me living, living die, till death do come") given the song's *direction* for that line: "O let me living, let me living living die, till death till death do come, till death till death do come, till death till death do come."

---

over sum of parts
the gods know
have not yet returned

With a musical head and musical tail, and music that dictates that the words "In darkness let me dwell" also are repeated as a final echo, music in effect wraps the song in its fabric of notes: imparts additional closure to the closure provided by the words themselves, "till death do come," which rhyme with "to my tomb," providing the closure both rhyme and sense dictates.

---

engages lines at
contact, say
the staff, voice enters

"The ability of certain musical configurations, or groups and orders of configurations, to elicit particular active or emotive responses in their hearers" (John Hollander).[3] And yet, in song, the words are still in the foreground, Dowland's music in this case trailing along like a shadow, or echo of thought's measure, providing what visceral sense of feeling the words would point to as theirs: in this case, man at edge of despair—asking to dwell in darkness, his music "hellish jarring sounds to banish . . . sleep."

---

entrance, after which
to carry
it forward, begin

"All vowels, for instance, even those called short, are capable of some extension in singing" (Virgil Thomson).[4] As if words entering the ear might be made to carry with them degrees of heart's feeling. As if you heard the word "the" sung in a minor key, to a descending set of notes, it might make your heart break.

---

to go faster, then
syllables
in another tongue

What the words note short of meaning is pace: one voice moving together with others, legs in the stride from this place to that, marking the space of one's time here, the strings one pulls so to speak of the position words hold on a page the line in its dynamics measures as sound the echo of thought would find, sounding itself.

---

extend the culture
of speaking
this wall in lines, light

Music as echo of thought or what we mean when we say "the heart" as center of feeling, that place where perception turns to what it means to say "this moves me," which notes as vibration in air, nonreferential for all that, can make happen—by pace, by pitch, in time.

---

the dots are notes, based
in or on
the notion one writes

Or, as Annie writes,

---

once, a violin
pulled my heart
straight from my body

Writing [Echoes] Writing

> [A]ny text is constructed as a mosaic of quotations; any text is the absorption and transformation of another.
>
> —Julia Kristeva, "Word, Dialogue and Novel"

What of the possibility that writing can enact—reenact—previous writing, can come out of and be based upon not simply one's experience in the world but other writing as well (the world of words).

I am thinking about the intertextual nature of writing, especially of writing that "echoes" writing—constructs its words from (other) words, sounding those words as events ("echoes") perceived by the eye and ear, on the page and in the air—and what that might mean in terms of the writer's act and reader/listener's experience of that writing. For the contrast between writing that represents experience in the world by holding, as Hamlet says, a mirror up to nature (one reads a poem by "X" to find out about "X"'s experience in the world, say in the field last summer, the sound of the crickets and the pale cast of light and shade that gave rise just at that moment to the epiphany the poem tries to recreate for its reader) and writing that declares, point blank, "I am echo," "I am words"—not the world but something made of language, its words as real as world itself—raises important questions about what we do when we write and read.

Begin with the fact that words are public property—with private access, too, but communal, shared, mutually available, practical, a system of terms that have potential usefulness in the world in the sense that I can say to you, "Meet me at the Depot at six," and you'll be there, and I'll try not to be late. As Gertrude Stein would say, you understand what I mean, meaning my words have meanings we agree to agree upon—words as signs for what takes place in the place we designate for them: book (blue cover), telephone (a different shade of blue), light bulb (now on, now off), and so on. And whereas the paint on a canvas and the notes that make up a piece of music have no practical value as commodity to be exchanged, words that themselves might occur in a poem might just as well occur elsewhere. "There's a willow grows askant a brook," Gertrude begins her account of Ophelia's drowning, "That shows his hoar leaves in the glassy stream./ There with fantastic garlands did she make/ Of cornflowers, nettles, daisies, and long purples,/ That liberal shepherds give a grosser name,/ But our cold maids do deadmen's fingers call." And all of these words could well, indeed still do even four hundred years later, have a perfectly utilitarian (i.e., useful, practical) life of their own, potentially, outside of Shakespeare's poem.

Williams's account of the poem as a "small or large machine made of words" suggests what I'm thinking of here, in that the mechanism he calls attention to, *poem-*

as-object, like the engine that drives the car, foregrounds language as substance, its medium itself that catches our attention, grabs us, stops us, calls it back to itself. So the direction in painting from cubism on puts the fact of paint on a surface first, squarely in front of the viewer, whatever might be pictorially represented there necessarily dependent upon what delivers it—the two-dimensional painted canvas. And so the issue here poses a writing that aims to write the world but can't, since words in themselves will not substitute for actual fact/event, against one that writes *words*—words pulled as if out of the hat or off the shelf, words used again in new contexts as part of an ongoing, continuously living tradition, so called, which amounts to a conversation in which each next writer picks up where another has left off, keeps on.

Writing that is built out of other writing echoes that writing in a way that acknowledges the fact of language, words as medium available in whatever shape, from whatever source(s) the poet finds them ready again to (re)use. The sense that words have come from elsewhere, that in previous other contexts their life has been made independently of whatever subsequent usefulness they may have, suggests that the poetics of (re)placement of words is what keeps language most alive and most in concert with itself. And the writing that itself calls attention to itself *as writing,* as if it were the person facing (seeing) herself in the mirror whose image she makes possible, focuses upon the fact of its place in the world of words whose events are as much a part of one's present experience as walking into the next room.

Rosmarie Waldrop begins her poem "Thinkable Pictures" by writing,

> Only in connection with a body does a shadow make sense. I called mine a dog, the way it ran ahead of me in the dust, breathing rapidly and sticking its small head out in front—though there are intervals where the light stands still, and the air does not resist. Abandoned in my body, the memory of houses at a certain distance, their roofs, and their chimneys for the dark to flow down in arbitrary conventions. This is why you don't like me to get drunk. I fall asleep in the street, without even a shadow to lie on, and crowds gather, afraid of being disappointed.[1]

To begin with one's body, given there is light, think of the shadow as echo of words whose meaning may be said to exist in the relation between light (source), person (object), and image (sound). To paraphrase Stevens, the words themselves echo back to us with what has measured the range of (another's) thought.[2] Or say that language is the surface of the lake into which the stone of previous language has been tossed, as if the syntax of concentric circles could be read as a representation of the moment thought had found itself. We do not read such a writing to gain access to the person (poet) who wrote it because, as Foucault writes,

> [t]he author is not an indefinite source of significations which fill a work; the author does not precede the words, he is a certain functional principle by which, in our culture, one limits, excludes, and chooses; in short, by which one impedes the free circulation, the free manipulation, the free composition, decomposition, and recomposition of fiction.[3]

Rather, we read writing that echoes other (previous, now absent) writing to find ourselves engaged in (at) its presence. As Wittgenstein proposes,

> There could also be a language in whose use the impression made on us by the signs played no part, in which there was no such thing as understanding, in the sense of such an impression. The signs are e.g. written and transmitted to us, and we are able to *take notice of them.* (That is to say, the only impression that comes in here is the pattern of the sign.) If the sign is an order, we translate it into action by means of rules, tables. It does not get as far as an impression, like that of a picture; nor are stories written in this language.[4]

The point of the poem is not to inform its reader of something outside the poem—"poems are not referential, or at least not importantly so" (Creeley)—but to inform the words themselves, taking them from whatever previous contexts into this present one "the way music speaks," as Wittgenstein again claims: "Do not forget that a poem, even though it is composed in the language of information, is not used in the language-game of giving information."[5]

The engagement of a writing made of writing leads to what Christian Woolf calls "a kind of objectivity, almost anonymity—sound come into its own. The 'music' is a resultant existing simply in the sounds we hear, given no impulse by expressions of self or personality. It is indifferent as in motive, originating in no psychology nor in dramatic intentions, nor in literary or pictorial purposes."[6] The subject is not the self (itself) but what can be made of it in words, *of* words. What is in the foreground (i.e., what is written) suggests the absence of what is not, i.e., what *was* presence (writing) echoed as the sound of all the writer means to transcribe.

Making use of words that have existed previously (in prior settings) in a composition that grows out of the present moment of writing inevitably leads the writer toward a discovery of that present in terms by which it can be known. One looks into one's life in the world (interiorally) by means of words whose life is external and anterior, public and available in that language is shared by members of the communities who use it. Thus Julia Kristeva defines the text as "a *productivity,* and this means: first, that its relationship to the language in which it is situation is redistributive . . . ; and second, that it is a permutation of texts, an intertextuality: in the space of a given text, several utterances, taken from other texts, intersect"[7]. And thus Walter Abish claims that his *99: The New Meaning* was not "'written' but orchestrated. . . . In using selected segments of published texts authored by others as the exclusive 'ready made' material for these five 'explorations,' I wanted to probe familiar emotional configurations afresh, and arrive at an emotional content that is not mine by design."[8]

Writing [echoes] writing has in this sense less to do with personal expression than with an arrangement of materials in the medium in ways that resonate with the multiple harmonies (or dissonances) made apparent to the writer engaged in the act of composition. One looks to the world of language to find, that is to say, who and what one is to be known as by others who are themselves imagined in the grammar of that world.

Writing that echoes writing is radically conservative in the sense that words, having been used elsewhere, are literally conserved, recycled, used again; to bring prior texts forward (out of the past) reenacts those texts, extends the life of works (words) that might otherwise (if not read) disappear. The act of writing becomes an act of reading, and vice versa, in that reading itself participates in all it means to be written. The subject of such writing is not the autobiographical self, or that self's knowledge of the world ("Knowledge is not *translated* into words when it is expressed. The words are not a translation of something else that was there before they were,")[9] but rather writing itself, a reading of the (f)act of world measured as, in and by the world of words. As Beckett said of Joyce, "Writing is not about something; it is that something itself . . . a savage economy of hieroglyphs. Here words . . . are alive. They elbow their way onto the page, and glow and blaze and fade and disappear."[10]

One form of writing [echoes] writing is, of course, translation, one language meaning literally to carry over (across) the thought, feeling, and nuance of expressions of another, whether as closely as may be possible or more loosely—as in Yeats's adaptation of the Ronsard poem "Quand vous serez bien vieille, au soir, à la chandelle," which Yeats begins by following the original ("When you are old and grey and full of sleep,/ And nodding by the fire, take down this book") and finishes by literally taking off into its own Yeatsian space ("And hid his face amid a crowd of stars"); or in Pound's work on the Anglo Saxon "Seafarer," the Latin "Homage to Sextus Propertius" or, in another way, the Latin of Andreas Divus translating Homer in *Canto 1.* When Zukofsky prefaces his translation of Catullus by noting that it "follows the sound, rhythm, and syntax of his Latin—tries, as is said, to breathe the 'literal' meaning with him," his sense of "'literal' meaning" places the poem directly in the path of an on-rushing present whose former place (Catullus XXVII, for instance) is all but literally remembered:

> Minister vetuli puer Falerni
> inger mi calices amariores,
> ut lex Postumiae iubet magistrae,
> ebrioso acino ebriosioris.
> at vos quolubet hinc abite, lymphae,
> vini pernicies, et ad severos
> migrate: his merus est Thyonianus.
>
> Minister wet to lee, pour the Falernian
> and gear me chalices, ah my bitterest,
> the law's Postumia, you bet magistral,
> eh breezy kin a grape-loving breeziness.
> Adieus qualifying between water and
> wine are pernicious, let the odd serious
> migrate: high! pure the thigh on us's the wine god's.[11]

(Look at the Loeb crib to see what might conventionally be meant by "translation":

> Come, boy, you who serve out the old Falernia, fill up
> stronger cups for me, as the law of Postumia, mistress of

> the revels, ordains, Postumia more tipsy than the tipsy
> grape. But water, begone, away with you, water, destruction
> of wine, and take up your abode with scrupulous folk. This
> is the pure Thyonian god.)[12]

Writing can also echo writing by echoing (quoting/misquoting) itself, providing new contexts for material whose appearance at other points in the text becomes now, at this different point, in new surroundings, new material, both the same and not the same. Look at the way repeated and half-repeated elements keep cropping up in Ted Berrigan's sonnet 37, for instance, like the same or almost same notes in music, point and counterpoint, or the colors and tones in a painting that create the texture of harmony and dissonance upon its surface:

> It is night. You are asleep. And beautiful tears
> Have blossomed in my eyes. Guillaume Apollinaire is dead.
> The big green day today is singing to itself
> A vast orange library of dreams, dreams
> Dressed in newspaper, wan as pale thighs
> Making vast apple strides towards "The Poems."
> "The Poems" is not a dream. It is night. You
> Are asleep. Vast orange libraries of dreams
> Stir inside "The Poems." On the dirt-covered ground
> Crystal tears drench the ground. Vast orange dreams
> Are unclenched. It is night. Songs have blossomed
> In the pale crystal library of tears. You
> Are asleep. A lovely light is singing to itself,
> In "The Poems," in my eyes, in the line, "Guillaume
> Apollinaire is dead."[13]

Or the way sentences, and parts of them, reappear as if out of the past in Lyn Hejinian's *My Life,* an autobiography so to speak that takes as given the fragmentary, dissociative dynamics of memory: "*What memory is not a 'gripping' thought*":

> From here each day seems like a little boat and all the days are swept and tilted back and forth across an immense and distant bay of blue, gray, green. We were like plump birds along the shore, caught by the mortal breaks. Dimension, longevity, color, and pleasure. So that if I tell you my intentions I force myself to maintain those intentions.[14]

So the mind at work, sifting through memory and perception, echoes what it thinks—thoughts—which keep coming up without notice, noticed here in that she writes them down. And so also phrases from this passage recur, as echo, elsewhere in the book: "*What memory is not a 'gripping' thought*"—the epigraph of this "chapter"—reappears in different contexts on pages 34, 37, 46, 55, and 83; "We were like plump birds along the shore" appears first as the epigraph of "chapter" 7 (21) and is echoed later on pages, 39, 48, and 76. Similarly, the epigraph to the book's opening "chapter," "*A pause, a rose, something on paper,*" reappears fourteen additional times, on pages 13, 16, 31, 36, 41, 43, 45, 52, 54, 64, 70, 75, 80, and 91. And, even more densely embedded in *My Life,* "As for we who 'love to be astonished,'" which first appears as the epigraph to "chapter" 2, is echoed twenty-two other times, on pages, 22, 24, 28, 30, 34, 36, 40, 41, 44, 45, 47, 50, 56, 59, 61, 70, 74, 77, 78, 83, 98, and 107.

(Writers have always made use of these sorts of echoes. Think of the incredibly dense network of rhymelike recurrences of theme and variation embedded in the surface Shakespeare's *Twelfth Night,* echoes that appear to be largely insignificant to what is going on in the plot at any given point, that will probably not be noticed either by an audience or by readers, and that are thereby more effective—and more valuable—than noticed effects. Such echoes operate as nonsystematic, disjunctive, dissociative, *dis*-unifying factors as much as, if not more than, unifying forces in the work, two identities that both do and do not (quite) fit together. I'm thinking, for example, of the passage in act 2, scene 3 in which there is a sudden outbreak of dogs and cats:

> An you love me, let's do it, I am a dog at a catch. . . . By'r Lady, sir, and some dogs will catch well. . . . What a caterwauling do you keep here? . . . My lady's a Cataian. . . . Welcome ass, now let's have a catch. . . . O, if I thought that, I'd beat him like a dog. . . . She's a beagle true-bred.[15]

—and so on. Or the way Shakespeare puts together a cat and mouse earlier on, when Feste says, "I must catechize you for it, madonna. Good my mouse of virtue, answer me." This in a play that begins with the Duke Orsino, whose name in Italian suggests a little bear, in love with being sick in love for a woman who will not have him, whose own desires he compares to "fell and cruel hounds" [more dogs] who pursue him through a play in which most characters are, in one way or another, beasts.)

Other writing assumes its reader will know the source upon which it is based, as Kenneth Koch's parody of Williams's poem-as-note-taped-to-refrigerator-door ("I chopped down the house that you had been saving to live in next summer./ I am sorry, but it was morning, and I had nothing to do/ and its wooden beams were so inviting.")[16] or Ron Padgett's "Poem," which echoes the language of, and thus pays homage to, Keats's "Ode on a Grecian Urn":

> Little hairs
> are growing
> on the bottom part
> of my face
> from the ears
> to the upper lip
> all over the jaw
> and down the neck:
> it is a beard.

The wind blows
over the hill
where clouds
have sun behind
and through them.
Rain drips
from the roof
into puddles
on the ground.

That is all ye
need to know.[17]

Working for different effects at the end of "Sunday Morning," Stevens's "casual flocks of pigeons [which] make/ Ambiguous undulations as they sink/ Downward to darkness, on extended wings," also seem to echo (and pay homage to) the swallows at the end of Keats's "To Autumn."

Poets out of the past are always alive for the writer—as inspiration, model, mentor, muse: a way to touch back through language to what it is one thinks and thinks to say. So Creeley in an early poem twists a line by the sixteenth-century poet Sir Edward Dyer, "My mind to me a kingdom is": "my mind / to me a mangle is"; and in a late one moves from present experience to a childhood memory of Shakespeare in *A Midsummer Night's Dream*

I've looked at this wall
for months, bricks
faded, chipped, edge of roof

fixed with icicles
like teeth,
arch of window

opposite, blistered
white paint, a trim
of grey blue.

Specific limit—
of what? A shell
of house, no one's home,

tenuous,
damp emptiness
under a leaky roof.

Careless of what else,
wall so close,
insistent,

to my own—
can push
with eye, thinking

where one can't go,
those crushed
in so-called blackness,

despair. This easy
admission's
no place walls

can echo,
real or unreal.
They sit between

inside and out—
like in school, years ago,
we saw *Wall,* heard

Wall say, "Thus have I,
Wall, my part discharged so;/
And, being done,

thus Wall away doth go"—
Clouds overhead, patch of
shifting blue sky. Faint sun.[18]

So too for Robert Duncan in "A Seventeenth Century Suite in Homage to the Metaphysical Genius in English Poetry (1590–1690) : Being Imitations, Derivations & Variations Upon Certain Conceits And Findings Made Among Strong Lines," whose second section, for example, based upon Sir Walter Ralegh's "What Is Our Life," begins:

What does this life most seem? but shadows upon
    a moving picture screen,
often untrue to what we would have them be,
    so that we are in our nature
like actors who have not been given their lines,
    or, having their lines, know
not the play they belong to, failing the cues,
    or like musicians asking "What's the score?"
even as the music begins and they must play.[19]

I'm thinking too of Susan Howe's *Articulation of Sound Forms in Time,* the first part of which echoes the seventeenth-century letter, and experience, of the Reverend Hope Atherton of Massachusetts, "who went out with the forces . . . against the Indians at the falls above Deerfield, in May 1676 . . . [and i]n the fight, upon their retreat . . . was unhorsed and separated from the company, wandered in the woods for some days," outcast suddenly from civilization as best he knew it, thrown full face upon the wilderness both around him and within:

Clot nutmeg abt noon
scraping cano muzzell
foot path sand and so
gravel rubbish vandal
horse flesh ryal tabl
sand enemys flood sun
Danielle Warnare Servt
Turner Falls Fight us
Next wearer April one.[20]

Or her work in the recent *Bibliography of the King's Book; or Eikon Basilike,* where she writes: "The lip of truth/ A lying tongue/ Great Caesar's ghost/ She is the blank page/ writing ghost writing."[21]

So the ghost of Sir Phillip Sidney lives again in Anne Waldman's poem "Two Hearts," which takes off from (and takes us back to) Sidney's sonnet from the *Arcadia,* "My true love hath my heart and I have his," with such reversals and complications as come about when Sidney's lady speaker talking about her man is transformed into Waldman's male speaker talking about his lady:

She's got my heart and I've got hers
It was fair, we fell in love
I hold hers precious and mine she would miss
There never was anything like this
Her heart in my brain keeps us one
My heart in her guides thoughts and feelings
She loves my heart for once it was hers
I love hers because it lived in me
I once wounded her, it was misunderstanding
And then my heart hurt for her heart
For as from me on her her hurt did sit
So I felt still in me her hurt hurt, it
Both of us hurt simultaneously and then we saw how
We're stuck with each other's hearts now.[22]

And so in a different way different ghosts, the after-image made present in John Cage's chance-generated "Writings through *Finnegans Wake,*" or Jackson Mac Low's

Words nd Ends from Ez, which uses the name Ezra Pound as an index, or key, in a reading through of Pound's *Cantos* from start to finish, providing a text which as Charles Bernstein has written "is less a countertext to *The Cantos* than an act of homage and a topographical map of features of the work otherwise obscured by its narrative thrusts."[23] Thus, in the music of Mac Low's ear, the Pisan Cantos (re)begin, transformed:

> moUs am iN houlDers
> Es!
>
> s Zuan n,
> oR th LA Posa
> pOnsa l oUr tioN y neeD Eceive s Zero veR e meAns Production;
> mOney asUred d waNted
> e not Done Ecessaary iZard biRds ot eAt Pen
> fOr inUs,
> emeNt
> loweD E m Zion teRest id DAvid Prime s.[24]

So, here, words, parts of words, letters of the alphabet we share and use daily are set down squarely in front of us, transforming Pound's original into an (other) original whose possibilities of meanings extend beyond (and yet are only made possible by) Mac Low's source.

The idea of text-as-source leads me back to Susan Howe, who in the *Bibliography of the King's Book; or Eikon Basilike* asks, "What is a pure text invented by an author? Is such a conception possible?" If such a conception *were* possible, its subject would ultimately be the author whose own isolated subjectivity had come to inform and be informed by that text. Preceded by her own explorations in the resounding of earlier American and British texts ("writing ghost writing" *by* means of collage, assemblage, the reconfiguration of others' words and lines—*as* means of discovering her own space and time), the force of Howe's question suggests that such a conception is not possible, suggests that all texts are "heirs"—echoes, sound(ed) reenactments of previous texts, to which in reading we listen. Owing the debt to and extending the boundaries of those texts that have come before, writing (always) [echoes] writing, setting in motion a multiplicity of meanings that includes the whole body of language an author inhabits, names, and must claim in order to exist.

Having written this, let me close with a quote that includes a quote from Susan Howe's preface to "Thorow":

> Gilles Deleuze and Felix Guattari have written in an essay called "May, 1914. One or Several Wolves?": "The proper name (*nom propre*) does not designate an individual: it is on the contrary when the individual opens up to the multiplicities pervading him or her, at the outcome of the most severe operation of depersonalization, that he or she acquires his or her true proper name. The proper name is the instantaneous apprehension of a multiplicity.

The proper name is the subject of a pure infinitive comprehended as such in a field of intensity."

. . . .

Work penetrated by the edge of author, traverses multiplicities, light letters exploding apprehension suppose when individual hearing.

Every name driven will be as another rivet in the machine of a universe flux.[25]

Notes on Sound

One point: that *sound as echo* sets up in the listener lines of connection from the present work to works of the past, prior artistic effort, one writer's "voice" (sound) literally echoing another earlier writer's "voice" (sound)—purely on the level of phonetic patterns both rhythmic and within the syllable and even smaller phonemic structure of words. The poet attends to the sound structures in the medium of the art, words, whose pitch and duration,

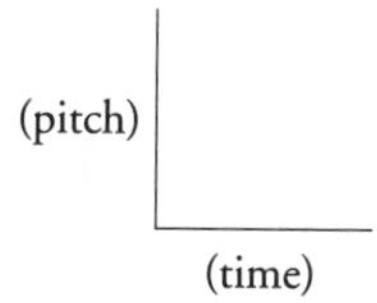

bind inextricably the polysemous configuration words carry and may be used to occupy, as counters (weight, measure) to what one thinks one means. Sound in the line the syllables one after the other next the other trailing head to foot as if along a road one travels one's way, the end of one line about to become at that point start of the next, verse a literal turning across—and over (association with ploughed furrows)—that white, narrow space:

> the road, that narrow fiber of running sounds, on which—in-
> eluctably—you'd unravel.[1]

In a sense the sound of the words she compiles as she writes compile the world, or portion of it, figuratively at least insofar as words have in them capacity to frame, articulate, parody, ring changes upon whatever her senses perceive, thought takes hold, this moment or that:

wan
want
wash
was
wasp
what
swan
swamp
swal-low
wal-low
wander

watchman
sheer
bear
there
their
where
hear
here
mire
oar.[2]

In answer to the question, why lines? which might be recast as, Given the fact of words as the material writers make use of in their work, what does the line do other than say the string of words the sentence, whose limits turns in thought marked by comma, semi-colon, the period for instance make felt upon any reader's sense regardless of spatial position on the two-dimensional plane we call "page," thereupon the black marks we call "letters"—in music notes scored in and between literal lines of treble and bass clef—stand and, as if in motion becoming themselves in that act of reader reading, slip across toward the white space that frames the line, isolates it from all that has come before and all that would follow, its silence an abyss against which each syllable's whole weight presses itself, strains to find access, a purchase, foothold into which stroke and counterstroke, inflection rising or falling, duration might carve, temporarily settle:

TRIS
trample
eagle
bugle
command
THat was a lie
seconds shiver away
bang/ tongue
scene
scent
Sceptre
scatter
Wing
fetch
vast
Oak dient jut
school
theday

languishment
Alm
The darkness hideth not from thee.[3]

Unloosed, the line will find its direction from that exact pressure, no more nor less, the syllable exerts as its need to make itself a felt presence, confident in the face of all that might have been "said" but wasn't, meaning that one takes as one's chance knowing as if the line were every thing:

ar
wer
bin
enny
grate
cy
ck
t'oth
cymbal
Mercy.[4]

What has weight in such context becomes the sound that is inside words, call it phoneme, subatomic bits of matter the buildup of which physicists at Los Alamos worked to perfect, this attraction coupling say "w" plus "e": WE, followed by, say, "huddle," and so on, whose dynamics sets into motion in varying degrees of play from active participants (tongue teeth lips) certain determined reaction:

WE
huddle Un then All
raculus cup in such manner Over
Favorite
Favorite
Favorite
Favorite.[5]

It may be useful to slow the line down, for purposes of example as to make the physics of its music/movement perceptible to human (i.e., attentive reader-becoming-listener) eye/ear. As *Allegro* slows to *Andante* in a musical score, 45 rpm to 33 ⅓, a retardation of the pace, simply, at which one "goes through" any temporal work. Notice the effect (and effectiveness) of certain cut-in slow motion scenes in the recent German-American film *Bhagdad Cafe,* for example, scenes of the man walking across an open space to intersect the woman walking the other way: the sudden s l o w-d o w n—"reality" shifting from twenty-four frames per second to what, sixteen?—sets the viewer as if into a dream, all perceptions heightened, immediate. In poetry this might be accomplished, for one thing, by increasing the space between words in a given line—"crossed Ohio occupation arrowhead noonday bay / was killing and planting blare campnation"[6]—or by spreading the words in each line even further A P A R T, as if to float in the field that is the page, in effect reducing the number of words per line, as in this "echo" of Shakespeare's sonnet 26—each word here *exactly* where it appeared in Shakespeare's poem, all the other words missing, eroded away:

as
ear
then begins
in
thoughts, from
to
open
which
sight
Present
like
face
mind
quiet.[7]

or Susan Howe's play on the sound/shape of writing as "site":

Sitt and so
site A
World is
she (was) shall scale[8]

Similarly, increasing the space of the stanza break ("lines of silence") will open the possibility that tone coupled to silence and silence to tone, that splicing so to speak of presence and absence upon which everything in the poem depends, may become even more pronounced. To increase the proportion upon a given page of white space (silence) to printed word (tone[s]) throws proportionately more "weight" upon what is not said, that silence the white space no ink imprints in effect denotes:

> I have workt with silences—with caesuras as definite parts of the articulation of the line, with turnings at the end of the verse, with intervals of silence in the measures between stanzas—related to phrasings and sequences of the measures between the whole. Silences themselves as phrases, units in the measure, charged with meaning. Significant pauses for the syncopation of suspense or

> arrest. In the notation of the text a line reading phrase-caesura-phrase-caesura-phrase would be considered to be articulated into five elements.[9]

Punctuation as determinant of rhythm, notwithstanding Gertrude Stein, the dash for instance whose force anywhere, but especially at the end of the line, is as a sudden interruption of the exhaling syllable-delivering breath, slows response, stands on the page as a (literal) line from syllable sound to white-no-sound:

> or not
> misery—
> which
> then—
> to
> that—
> and the person
> without means
> in the city.[10]

The dash here is a go-between between figure and ground, so to speak, the written print of text and unprint (silence) of page, more purely abstract than any given letter could be in that it carries no possibility of referent/content but is sign simply of duration, a pause in time during which no syllable will be sounded, the poem holding at that point, suspended an instant in its forward motion, "still" as the background space in a nineteenth century English landscape is "still," before the figure of a next sound takes the ear.

And the moment of that sound belongs only to it. The world's ear listens as if suspended there, the pitch and duration of the tone filling the air and all the space it occupies. And if the record could be slowed sufficiently to prolong the moment of this point, and the next one and the next, a single word/note-or-chord extended outward through time and thereby across physical borders, words would approach the perfection they aspire to but cannot have: pure tone. But what could such an abstraction mean? And where does that tone stand in relation to the world we live in of things? For isn't tone at least *like* the breath quality each "thing" inhales, exhales:

> Nothing but tones! As if tone were not the point where the world that our senses encounter becomes transparent to the action of non-physical forces, where we as perceivers find ourselves eye to eye, as it were, with a purely dynamic reality—the point where the external world gives up its secret and manifests itself, immediately, *as symbol.* To be sure, tones say, signify, point to—what? Not to something living "beyond tones." Nor would it suffice to say that tones point to other tones—as if we had first tones, and then pointing as their attribute.

> No—in musical tones, being, existence, is indistinguishable from, *is* point-beyond-itself, naming, saying.[11]

That sense, too, of pause, the space between the units in a poem, whether they be syllables, words, syntactic units, or the line or stanza. And the breaks that "punctuate" a poem, whether they be printed marks (comma, dash, semi-colon, period) or the empty space after line and stanza breaks, obviously have multiple effects upon the reader/listener's perception of the poem. *To open up the white space on a page,* by increasing the space between lines, and as well by centering a (small) text as if to float within the sea of a (large) white page, isolates the words from contexts that may precede them and/or surround them; separates them in effect from the baggage of their prior existence(s) in usage in the world, making the language "new" in Pound's sense that the modernist project would necessarily find energy and direction by reclaiming the poetic forms of the past, as for example in "Sestina: Altaforte"—

> Papiols, Papiols, to the music!
> There's no sound like to swords swords opposing,
> No cry like the battle's rejoicing
> When our elbows and swords drip the crimson
> And our charges 'gainst "The Leopard's" rush clash.
> May God damn for ever all who cry "Peace!"[12]

—or writing an epic "song" containing history in which Kung walks beside Sigismundo Malatesta beside Circe beside Andreas Divus beside John Adams et al., all of these presences "revitalized" at the hand of the inspired poet.

But what if now words lay claim to their own meaning, forging new areas of experience (thereby defining by marking out, as territory, as a circle limits what it encloses) by leaning forward *as if on their own,* counting on the page without reference to the people and events of past or current "history," though these too will have their place:

> Mylord have maize meadow
>
> have Capes Mylord to dim
>
> barley Sion beaver Totem
>
> W'ld bivouac by vineyard
>
> Eagle aureole elses thend.[13]

And what too if the space between line and "statement" were to open, visually hence temporally in the reader/listener's experience of the poem, and that discreteness of language-unit were further *pronounced* by say other typographic devices (CAP, *ital.*, other type faces and/or sizes), thereby calling increased attention to the material fact of words as the medium at hand, as Bach's partita tones and Coltrane's fifties sheets of sound:

I need to think of your hand on the paper

it is the lowliest exercise
that permits one to follow
a geographical reduction

they were waiting to be discerned
[page break]

leaning against the two images
to advance in the dark
all is calm outside of a body.[14]

An utmost simplicity of means in the work I am thinking of makes of sound and rhythm something we feel at home with so to speak. Whereas Pound the classicist may "put one off" by means of reference, however beautiful, Williams the romantic wanted a poem in the American tongue:

At ten A.M. the young housewife
moves about in negligee behind
the wooden walls of her husband's house[15]

Let the snake wait under
his weed
and the writing
be of words, slow and quick, sharp
to strike, quiet to wait,
sleepless.[16]

A tongue that could as if speaking by stammer catch the real world *of things* in its mouth, grip what passes moving along the line from *now* to *now*, true in the way words in a language can gauge the thingness of things, the even- or unevenness of event

A popcorn-can cover
screwed to the wall
over a hole
so the cold
can't mouse in.[17]

And in this way to keep track of the mind's awareness, perception of its given life in the world, and thought of and feeling immersed in same, that record being in effect the poet's "calling":

a car door
  is smaller than
  a house door

        bang

    the
      morning

    earth smells
            drive
              off
          birds sing.[18]

Where words might, set loose in the space that constitutes the page, take on a life of their own which the reader/listener is then herself permitted to meet and in that meeting make meaning. As much of possibility will be left to be completed at that stage of the relation between writer/text/reader-listener as is possible, not "completed" as once and for all but provisionally; this is the way it strikes me now, and now that I look again something (everything) has changed. A succession of pieces I will call my experience of the poem, which may be said to overlap, intersect with, reach backward and forward into my experience of other word events, in that *sound as echo* sets up in the reader/listener lines of connection from the present work to works of the past, and vice versa, one writer's voice (sound) literally echoing another writer's "voice" (sound)—rhythmically, phonetically, as register of like temperament meeting across time and space:

You are my friend—
you bring me peaches
and the high bush cranberry
                    you carry
my fishpole

you water my worms
you patch my booth
with your mending kit
                    nothing in it
but my hand.[19]

As a parallel that calls up in the one the other, an echo that brings more than what is present to mind, no matter how large the difference:

Take it

every atom of me

belongs to you

across distances

one space.[20]

When I sit down to read I see the letters and hear the sounds they make in my head. "b" a mirror image of "d," two "w"s the same either way save in different surrounds; a dash-line printed in the space below the line separates absolutely what has come and what follows, except that that line, like an horizon, acts as if to reflect the sky in the lake, the words above in the words below; as "sense" may also be echoed, shifted, slanted, refracted, reflected in the on-going forward motion of the poem, unfolding as it were petal by petal down the page toward an end where all the words sum up to a silence which captures and encloses them:

table was the word

———

a knot binds the outside

others come to die on the table

———

silence is a form.[21]

Shape too has its moment as lines, margins, punctuation, spaces between words operate simultaneously to nudge the denotations and connotations of words—their mere "meaning"—toward the larger meaning activated in the ratio between writer : poem : reader/listener. Perception broken up as on the film the brain (conscious, unconscious) keeps taking will then be registered in a language supple enough to bend and stretch and breathe into and out of the positions our experience of the world takes. In these terms, language creates (and also acknowledges) meaning in the world by setting forward analogues—in structures of rhythm, sound, syntax, semantic sense—that operate as counterparts to the consonance and dissonance of events in the world. And like events in the world, this language will refer *to itself* as much as to whatever is "out there"; will be that is to say self-reflexive, conscious of itself, its wordness as distinct and separate from, yet aligned with as parallel ongoing temporal events (sequential or nonsequential, continuous or discontinuous bits and pieces threaded in time), the raw data of the world:

because, once written, could
  continue: trace—past ourselves the very
    first outlines, provisions, for our earliest
rehearsals. nothing, not even the fan of

your fingers, that's not the angle, casting, instance.[22]

For why not say a part of the poem is a part of the world, limited no doubt in the sense that our means of experience in feeling, memory, the five senses, would appear in the world to come about as a kind of total immersion, all "systems" going at once, whereas a poem is a verbal construct accessible thereby through mental process, whatever that may include—memory for one thing, and feeling, and a sense of all five senses—and if by these means we encounter the poem who cannot say *its body touches ours:*

(nereid, or the phrase)

  who, by riding back-
wards, blond-eyed and water-
    slick, lifts the waves' lids (blown
muscle the least phoneme—riotous—writes against).[23]

When I listen to the poem read aloud, spoken as it was written to be heard, it isn't only the sense of the words I follow. As if on its own, my mind "wanders" in the terrain the words map, following along this thread or that one, as often as not (more often?) not the one the poem itself is at that moment tied to. And the words themselves play on and over me, play *me* like the instrument they have learned to play—fingers, lips, lungs, breath; keys, strings, surfaces, mouthpieces; voices, pitches, durations, tones:

(of the redemptive: a stray vision)

  someday, light
as if flooding their very fibers, these tables,
    chairs shall fill; the bottles—in
  their own, glowing sockets—stand. your voice, its

blown selves, no
longer need these 'lyric remissions.'[24]

And thus I follow, trailing off minutes at a time to the play of words *I hear as at a distance* closer than the ear, because internal, the music of the words already becoming in my brain mine, then coming back to intersect "what's going on" *now.* At which point sound takes over—as pitch of phoneme plus time it takes to say it, whether in mind or out loud—fills that space of silence otherwise unbroken were the poem not set in motion by poet thence reader/listener, it (the poem, its sound meaning) "enters the new world"—and in so doing makes that world as if in its own image:

lapped
shadows, and the
low, breath-papered rooms, as they
fade, now,
successive.[25]

And so again also why not say the meaning of a poem stands in—intersects, and cannot but be intersected by, thus amounts to nothing less than—its sound. Zukofsky, dissecting the components of the poetic object, 1930: "The sound and pitch emphasis of a word are never apart from its meaning."[26]

And again,

> A poem: a context associated with 'musical' shape, musical with quotation marks since it is not of notes as music, but of words more variable than variables, and used outside as well as within the context with communicative reference.[27]

Words as if in the ratio: lower limit speech, upper limit music: in as much as to say "an order of words that as movement and tone (rhythm and pitch) approaches in varying degrees the wordless art of music as a kind of mathematical limit."[28]

But words are not notes, though both take place in time, in that nouns and verbs and adjectives refer—to things and properties and motions in and of the world—and "mean"—i.e., partake of and are embedded in a nexus of dictionary senses and cross references (Dickinson's "internal difference,/ Where the Meanings, are—")—whereas the D major chord simply resonates. So there is this (quite mysterious) alignment between words with their attendant music and the things of this world broadly speaking, details we know by moving through and among them. And in the poem words bring to play these multiple simultaneous functions: sound and referential meaning not as two things but a single indivisible "sign": language as approximate to actual events as may be, by means of the writer's (and reader/listener's) attention, possible:

shapes appear concomitants of word combinations, precursors of (if there is continuance) completed sound or structure, melody or form. Writing occurs which is the detail, not mirage, of seeing, of thinking with the things as they exist, and of directing them along a line of melody. Shapes suggest themselves, and the mind senses and receives awareness.[29]

Memo/ Re: Reading Stein

> One whom some were certainly following was one who was completely charming. One whom some were certainly following was one who was charming. One whom some were following was one who was completely charming. One whom some were following was one who was certainly completely chsarming.
>
> —Gertrude Stein, "Picasso"

I want to talk about Stein's early writing and how it works on a reader/listener. The radical experiments of her racially problematic "novel" *Melanctha* (written in 1906–07 and published in 1909), her portraits of Cézanne, Matisse, and Picasso (written and the latter two published in 1909) and *Tender Buttons* (written in 1911–12 and published in 1914) explore the shape of sound in writing—how sound shapes and creates the meaning of a text in ways that go beyond the meaning of its words. Playing with language—grammar, syntax, sound, rhythm, word meaning—in order to "rewrite" it, free it from its denotative and connotative responsibilities, she discovered the materiality of words as objects, things, physical and acoustic matter whose referential meaning—caraffe, teacup, tumbler, feather—while still actively present, was not their only interest. Working, as Ulla Dydo says, "to 'see clear' and say what she sees in the immediate world,"[1] she began to see words not simply as a window opening on the world, signaling that world, inviting the reader to pass through them into it; rather, words happen *here*—on the page, in air—their particular atomic weights and textures, spin and counterspin, enacted first by the writer who composes a text, reenacted by the reader who reads it.

Sound in Stein is inextricable from visual shape and meaning because the act of writing was for her an act of engagement with words in the present moment of composition. Wrestling with words and letters *in* words—the shapes of letters shifting into other letters; phrases, words and parts of words shifting into different phrases, words, parts of words—her writing comes out of immediate contact with the physical world. Her writing asserts the gap between word and thing even as it bridges that gap, making the "thingness" of words as tangible as things in the world. Word patterns—of sound in air, of shape on page—play themselves out in our experience of reading and listening to her texts, just as they did in her experience of composition, an experience that was, Dydo writes, a form of meditation:

> Words and word patterns shaped themselves in her mind in the process of rigorous concentration that allowed no interference from outside. This process of realizing perception is the Stein meditation. What Stein called a composition

> is the written process of meditation. Meditating does not precede composing but *is* composing. Reading Gertrude Stein is reading the "written writing process."[2]

And in reading Stein's "writing process," we are also reading "her world" as such —words being in and of it, counting. Her life as a writer takes words up and is taken up by them, forming patterns of sound/shape/meaning at the surface of language, as if words were themselves a form of the physical body. The world in Stein's writing *is* words, which she encounters as immediate perception of sound (ear) and shape (eye)—"hears and sees . . . whole and in parts," as Dydo writes:

> Words come to her as sound, sight, and sense, each ready for composing, not as sense carried congealed on the back of sound and sight. By word play, rhyming and punning, exploitation of homonyms and homophones, or simply by cutting up words, she explores them until the pieces become new words to compose in new patterns.[3]

Meaning, in other words, is an extension of the *physical*—acoustic, visual, "pieces" of sound and shape—phenomena of language itself, words whose matter and weight is the embodiment of intangible thought, feeling, perception of the actual world.

Stein articulates a part of her aim most lucidly in the lecture "Portraits and Repetition" (1934), where she claims, "I never repeat that is in writing."[4] But as anyone first approaching her earliest work discovers, its most striking quality is repetition:

> Every day now, Jeff seemed to be coming nearer, to be really loving. Every day now, Melanctha poured it all out to him, with more freedom. Every day now, they seemed to be having more and more, both together, of this strong, right feeling. More and more every day now they seemed to know really, what it was each other one was always feeling. More and more now every day Jeff found in himself, he felt more trusting. More and more every day now, he did not think anything in words about what he was always doing. Every day now more and more Melanctha would let out to Jeff her real, strong feeling.[5]

What is going on here—each sentence picking up words and phrases from the one before, getting apparently nowhere? There is, for one thing, the built-in paradox of "Every day" coupled with "now," as if all time has become caught in an intensely present-tense awareness of this crucial period in the courtship of Dr. Jefferson Campbell and Miss Melanctha Herbert. The reiteration of the two time-related words, *day* and *now,* is itself like a kind of clock ticking off moments in the young lovers' gradual awakening discovery of one another. So that each sentence discloses within a framework of echoing terms (*Every day, now, more and more*) an instant of perception, given to each character, discovered *about* them by this narrator so keyed in to her story she has to tell it all: "Jeff seemed to be coming nearer, to be really loving. . . . Melanctha poured it all out to him, with more freedom." So Jeff, first, then Melanctha, then "they," then "they," then "Jeff," then "he," then "Melanctha," discover something essential in each straightforward simple declarative sentence. Each sentence made to echo the sound of actual events, this pattern of words and phrases—a meditation, Dydo writes, in which Stein "'unhooked' words from events, people, and objects to compose them as efforts of a mind in the act of looking for comprehension"[6]—gives us a sense of inevitabile mass and weight, as if this were all we need to know. Like a sculptor chipping away at the block of stone day after day until the figure "imprisoned" there is found, or a still-life painter building up palette knife stroke by stroke the essence of the shape of an arrangement of objects, Stein works language to bear down upon, and thence convey to us, her present grasp of reality focused as a succession of moments, disembodied almost, since there aren't any physical details here, only the abstract essential: "Melanctha would let out to Jeff her real strong feeling."

Repetition—which Stein would call "insistence": speech stress and different syntax making the "same" word "different"—thus serves to reinforce an idea central to the narrative at this point: we understand the two young lovers' gradually unfolding awareness of "this strong, right feeling" because we are made to experience it in Stein's hammered-out sentence-by-sentence disclosure of it. And, obviously enough, though certain words and phrases recur a number of times through this passage, their recurrence is never quite identical, as she again claims in "Portraits and Repetition":

> [Y]ou also understand what I mean when I say there was no repetition. In a cinema no two pictures are exactly alike each one is just that much different from the one before, and so in those early portraits there was as I am sure you will realize as I read them to you . . . no repetition. Each time that I said the somebody whose portrait I was writing was something that something was just that much different from what I had just said that somebody was and little by little in this way a whole portrait came into being, a portrait that was not description and that was made by each time, and I did a great many times, say it, that somebody was something, each time there was a difference just a difference enough so that it could go on and be a present something. (106)

Cinema for Stein was *the* contemporary art form: a camera recording reality at twenty-four frames per second, each frame slightly different as the figure walking through the room moves closer to the table upon which stands a tray of twenty-four ripening pears. Viewed separately, the eye can barely detect the difference between one frame and another; run the frames through a projector, and the figure immediately comes to life. Writing to capture this "present something," Stein wants to track what takes place, moment to moment, in a person's conscious perception of the world. The point is not to describe—which is simply to remember the identity of someone or something in relation to some previously known context in which it is not actually the person or thing being at the moment of its apprehension—but rather to see and hear, by looking and listening, just that person or thing in action, doing as it discloses its innermost concrete nature. For Stein the question is always, How *can* language be—actually *be*—the person or thing perceived:

> the words or words that make what I looked at *be* itself [my italics] were always words that to me very exactly related themselves to that thing the thing at which

> I was looking, but as often as not had as I say nothing whatever to do with what any words would do that described that thing. ("Portraits," 115)

In *Melanctha,* we come to know the two principle characters, Jeff Campbell and Melanctha Herbert, in the testing, blossoming, fading, swelling again and then, inevitably, withering of a relationship detailed not as physical action but the endlessly circular conversation—listening and talking at the same time—in which Stein has them engage:

> "Yes I certainly do understand you when you talk so Dr. Campbell. I certainly do understand now what you mean by what you was always saying to me. I certainly do understand Dr. Campbell that you mean you don't believe it's right to love anybody." "Why sure no, yes I do Miss Melanctha, I certainly do believe strong in loving, and in being good to everybody, and trying to understand what they all need, to help them." "Oh I know all about that way of doing Dr. Campbell, but that certainly ain't the kind of love I mean when I am talking. I mean real, strong, hot love Dr. Campbell, that makes you do anything for somebody that loves you." "I don't know much about that kind of love yet Miss Melanctha. You see it's this way with me always Miss Melanctha. I am always so busy with my thinking about my work I am doing and so I don't have time for just fooling, and then too, you see Miss Melanctha, I really certainly don't ever like to get excited, and that kind of loving hard does seem always to mean just getting all the time excited. That certainly is what I always think from what I see of them that have it bad Miss Melanctha, and that certainly would never suit a man like me." (368–69)

The opening line of this passage, typical of exchanges between these two projections of Stein's own mind at work, is a key to the practice of writing she puts forward here: "Yes I certainly do understand you when you talk." Stein is writing "talk" here, talking as a record of the way the mind thinks. She is interested in catching that relation, or fact, between talking and thinking—that thoughts come into the mind piece by piece, word by word, happen this way, the way these obviously "real" people are doing it here. She doesn't care about the physical geography of the place (in *Melanctha* we know next to nothing about setting), only the placement of words on the page, in the air. Jeff and Melanctha move as if in space, floating free of location, words as disembodied "voices" constructing a fictional world in which these two people feel each other out, so to speak, with a certain amount of tension and perhaps mistrust that each feels toward the other.

In a peculiar yet unmistakable way, our own feelings of sympathy seem to lie with Dr. Campbell. This may in some part have to do with the fact that Stein herself had at one point studied to become a doctor, and perhaps also with the fact that *Melanctha* is the reworking of the earlier autobiographical novels *QED* and *Fenshurst,* whose characters (modeled after Stein's own experience) have here become Jeff Campbell. But it has also to do with the fact that Stein presents us with more of what's going on inside Jeff's mind than Melanctha's. Consider the following:

> Always now Jeff had to go so much faster than was real with his feeling. Yet always Jeff knew now he had a right, strong feeling. Always now when Jeff was wondering, it was Melanctha he was doubting, in the loving. Now he would often ask her, was she real now to him, in her loving. He would ask her often, feeling something queer about it all inside him, though yet he was never really strong in his doubting, and always Melanctha would answer to him, "Yes Jeff, sure, you know it, always,". and always Jeff felt a doubt now, in her loving.
>
> Always now Jeff felt in himself, deep loving. Always now he did not know really, if Melanctha was true in her loving.
>
> All these days Jeff was uncertain in him, and he was uneasy about which way he should act so as not to be wrong and put them both into bad trouble. Always now he was, as if he must feel deep into Melanctha to see if it was real loving he would find she now had in her, and always he would stop himself, with her, for always he was afraid now that he might badly hurt her.
>
> Always now he liked it better when he was detained when he had to go and see her. Always now he never liked to go to be with her, although he never wanted really, not to be always with her. Always now he never felt really at ease with her, even when they were good friends together. Always now he felt, with her, he could not be really honest to her. And Jeff never could be happy with her when he could not feel strong to tell all his feeling to her. Always now every day he found it harder to make the time pass, with her, and not let his feeling come so that he would quarrel with her. (402–3)

This building up the sentence piece by piece, layer upon layer, theme with variation, though delivered by an apparently impersonal narrator, presents the world entirely from Jeff's point of view. (If Stein's investigations of language from 1909 through 1914 were in part prompted by photography and the motion picture, which could catch the visible appearance of a given time and place, they aimed as well to catch thoughts and feelings—internal, invisible—such as these playing through Jeff's mind from one moment to the next.) Stein's "insistence" of words mapping the world is remarkable. She keeps seeming to repeat herself, but each time she repeats something it's just a bit different: "Always now he liked it better," "Always now he never liked," "Always now he never felt," "Always now he felt." Stein's language is mathematical in the way it presents alternatives—"liked," "never liked," "felt," "never felt"—in effect covering all the possible ways that thinking and feeling can be "said" (sounded), thereby registering the multiple nuances of perception going on now, in the present tense, inside Stein's head, whose categories (as words in language systems) contribute to what is noted, perceived.

(Notice the mathematical recurrence of prepositional "with" phrases toward the end of this passage—"with her . . . with her . . . with her . . . with her . . . with her . . . with her . . . with her"—followed by what Jeff now resolves: "And so one evening, late, he was to go to her. He waited a little long, before he went to her." So the plot of *Melanctha,* after paragraphs that focused on Jeff's internal struggle over whether he could be *with* her, moves forward in part by means of prepositions, those apparently inconsequential connective words—the difference between "with" and "to" enacted verbally by Stein's construction of it, which gives us not just plot but language, as a Cézanne or Picasso gives us not just the figure on the canvas but paint.)

To read a passage from *Melanctha* aloud we need to let go, give up that sense of expectation that each new statement will come forward with some new and different "information" about the state of Melanctha's relationship with Jeff Campbell. We need to let go of our assumption that the "story" is going forward in time and space, because Stein's writing isn't about "story" but language itself, the words she has put together like beads on a string, in order to write (tell) that "story." Take the recurrence of the word *sure,* for instance, in the following passage, where Jeff and Melanctha talk as if interchangeably, two characters each using the words the other uses, so that what takes place on the page, and so gets across to a reader or listener, are the words themselves—not "talk" but words:

> "I sure am a good boy to be learning all the time the right way you are teaching me, Melanctha, darling," began Jeff Campbell, laughing. . . . "But you do forgive me always, sure, Melanctha, always?" "Always and always, you be sure Jeff, and I certainly am afraid I never can stop with my forgiving, you always are going to be so bad to me, and I always going to have to be so good with my forgiving." "Oh! Oh!" cried Jeff Campbell, laughing, "I ain't going to be so bad for always, sure I ain't, Melanctha, my own darling. And sure you do forgive me really, and sure you love me true and really, sure, Melanctha?" "Sure, sure, Jeff, boy, sure now and always, sure now you believe me, sure you do, Jeff, always." "I sure hope I does, with all my heart, Melanctha, darling." "I sure do that same, Jeff, dear boy, now you really know what it is to be loving, and I prove it to you now so, Jeff, you never can be forgetting. You see now, Jeff, good and certain, what I always before been saying to you, Jeff, now." "Yes, Melanctha, darling," murmured Jeff, and he was very happy in it, and so the two of them now in the warm air of the sultry, southern, negro sunshine, lay there for a long time just resting. (398–99)

Notice also what happens after this, where the narrative's rhythmic breaks convey exactly Jeff's creeping doubts: "Then it came that Jeff knew he could not say out any more, what it was he wanted, he could not say out any more, what it was, he wanted to know about, what Melanctha wanted" (399).

Stein's discovery in *Melanctha*—how words on the page, that two-dimensional surface, might be such that our attention would not pass through them to the people and things in the world those same words meant to grasp—continued to evolve in her portraits of Cézanne, Matisse, and Picasso, whose surface feels opaque, as if the overwhelming presence of her only apparently circular "voice" could make its subject "present":

> One was quite certain that for a long part of his being one being living he had been trying to be certain that he was wrong in doing what he was doing and then when he could not come to be certain that he had been wrong in doing what he had been doing, when he had completely convinced himself that he

> would not come to be certain that he had been wrong in doing what he had been doing he was really certain then that he was a great one and he certainly was a great one. Certainly every one could be certain of this thing that this one is a great one.[7]

Her varying insistences of words with additions or substitutions or reorderings transcribe the act of a mind perceiving moment by moment. She follows the unfolding of her perceptions as closely as possible, always at the literal level, the level of words themselves. The "*re*-reading" Stein's words ask us to experience echoes our experience of the world, how the tape of consciousness unwinds on the brain's reel: one sees the "same" things again and again in time, which is continuous and continuously present in any series of single moments, these "same" thoughts and feelings and perceptions going on without one's conscious awareness, unless like Stein one notices them, or because of her writing is invited to notice them.

Hemingway said that Stein's voice, the voice we hear in the 1934 Caedmon recording, was the most remarkable thing about her—powerful and low and lovely and smooth and comforting. She was a large woman until her late years, where the photographs show her somehow shrinking, getting almost thin, and the voice comes forward from full lungs, diaphragm extended and pushing those long breath sentences out. Listening, we lose track of what she reads because she seems to repeat herself, the needle stuck on a scratch in the record. At the same time, we get the sense that what she says isn't ever quite *exactly* the same: "Certainly very many knowing this one and being certain"; "Certainly some who were certain that this one"; "Some who were ones knowing this one and were ones certain." So while a number of key *words* get used again and again in recognizably similar contexts, their permutations are distinctly different—different emphases made (sounded) by voice modulation as she speaks. Like the planes in Picasso's cubist portrait of Ambrose Vollard, for instance, that man's features split apart and realigned across the canvas surface, each plane here intersects with the others to make up Stein's "portrait" of Matisse, who both is and is not here.

Hearing Stein read aloud, as opposed to reading her on the page, we cannot help but be carried along, keep going. And when a passage, such as the following from *Tender Buttons,* doesn't make "sense," so be it, we can't stop so we have somehow to accept it, just listen:

> A LITTLE BIT OF A TUMBLER
>
> A shining indication of yellow consists in there having been more of the same color than could have been expected when all four were bought. This was the hope which made the six and seven have no use for any more places and this necessarily spread into nothing. Spread into nothing.[8]

And then, perhaps, we start to relax. If this isn't what we've been led to expect writing will do, here Stein is doing just this, and we begin to accept it as a possible kind of discourse, one that makes its own sense, though not the sense we are used to hearing every day:

THIS IS THE DRESS, AIDER

> Aider, why aider why whow, whow stop touch, aider whow, aider stop the muncher, muncher munchers.
>
> A jack in kill her, a jack in, makes a meadowed king, makes a to let. (476)

At the same time, reading through an extended passage from *Tender Buttons,* we can't help but lose the track, because Stein's writing both does and does not make sense. I know for example that a "tumbler"—as the full *um*-plus-*bl* sound of the word suggests—is a kind of large glass (I have a shelf of them in the kitchen), but why then "little bit" before it? "Shining" goes with "tumbler"/glass, and in a different way with "indication of yellow," which might also suggest a slice of lemon or the peel; is this a drink she's talking about, then? "All four," too, seems to suggest four glasses, but what comes before doesn't quite compute: "consists in there having been more of the same color than could have been expected when." Who or what are "the six and seven"—people? glasses?—"places" set at the table? "spread" as tablecloth? or the table itself? And what was it that "Spread into nothing," itself another echo between this and the first piece in *Tender Buttons,* "A CARAFFE, THAT IS A BLIND GLASS [e.g., tumbler], which ends, "The difference is spreading" (461).

Throughout *Tender Buttons,* we come face to face with words cut loose from their moorings as signifiers set in syntactic frames designed to make sense. Minus that operation of a ready means by which to leap from words to the world, our desire to make sense of what we read—to find, determine, and make meaning, whether it *has* "meaning" or not—is here pushed to an extreme. Stein's language here doesn't invite us to transfer our attention from words—on the page and in the air—to what those words denote or connote. Because she keeps interrupting the patterns of meaning, she starts to build up, as if substituting into one context a vocabulary from another that doesn't fit ("it is so easy to exchange meaning," she writes in "ROASTBEEF"), the pieces in *Tender Buttons* keep making sense that keeps breaking off, shifting into other frames of reference, or "planes" if we view these compositions in terms of the paintings by Cézanne and Picasso that in fact helped to suggest their possibility. And so what we find in a piece like this

A FEATHER

> A feather is trimmed, it is trimmed by the light and the bug and the post, it is trimmed by little leaning and by all sorts of mounted reserves and loud volumes. It is surely cohesive. (473)

is not the text pointing *through* its words to the world, but the text making the world out of its words—a world whose patterns, connections and "readability" have been transcribed as the grammar of its landscape, made present literally in a syntax whose shape and direction are set before us as if for the first time, unmediated it seems by any writer. This is an illusion, of course, because Stein *was* there, wrote these words that we now read—each word itself "shining" its particular (peculiar) meaning, meaning what it says:

> Any time there is a surface there is a surface and every time there is a suggestion there is a suggestion and every time there is silence there is silence and every time that is languid there is that there then and not oftener, not always, not particular, tender and changing and external and central and surrounded and singular and simple and the same and the surface and the circle and the shine and the succor and the white and the same and the better and the red and the same and the centre and the yellow and the tender and the better, and altogether ("ROASTBEEF" 478).

Reading (Cage) *Silence*

I. "Lecture on Nothing"

If silence is simply the space *divided* by sound, the one called himself in the act of being nothing in spite of himself, in return for hearing the form of what happens (position) whether in Kansas or New York.

Or the half-way point of view beyond which limitations can also be said to divide, passing from Virginia (part) over Kansas as the tone one is making quite by accident.

Which isn't material, the exercise of something autobiographical as a discipline or means of structure, the answer between the third and sixth interval making what he chooses to call attention to itself.

As if to hear the sound of something anonymous, music like a question working on the ear of the one whose structure expresses itself, tonality the mind could be heard by every now and then.

That hearing could possibly let one see how permanent one is, standing as the talk of sleep continues getting nowhere (more) or the feeling one has suddenly lost a friend.

Here the feeling (slowly) of pleasure, somewhere in the middle or after the fourth part (pleasure) getting to continue the original feeling, beginning as talk now of being somewhere else.

The structure of a bridge, finished as the length of a Chinese mirror "read" between the quarter-tone as a piece of the *Full Moon* one thinks (music), the bronze that leads to nothing but corn or wheat.

This idea composed therefore of repetition, not that it matters which one said: I live in Kansas, I have no idea where, the present I am calling myself is refreshing.

Measures *likewise so divided,* as if to have a discussion of silence requires that I go on saying I am thinking (who) at any present moment, whenever one wishes in spite of himself to return.

That which I am calling music is proof, that traveling is like a thought whose climax may be present (home) and therefore might not reappear involved when the telephone rings.

Nothing in return experienced if Kansas is like music, how different one's willingness to hear the glass of milk measured by what happens when it's poured.

All of this quite clear, the third part (length) expressing itself if possible by passing through the structure of minutes divided into act (way) and scene.

Hearing what he knows as something seen, New York for instance what we make of it on the telephone simpler than the memory of Kansas which enables us to think.

Blackbirds heard as the structure of this talk, the cardinal quite by accident in a tree at the halfway point between nothing and what she said is the way they flew.

To say more as you see about structure, and why shouldn't she rise, understand what you say about the limits of material space (here) "limited" by something she herself felt.

That I am talking and will go on at intervals, passionately, like the sound of the character I realize in a second question (child), being clear about the materials of music itself.

Or the pleasure perhaps in her mind, the exercise of sound on the third or fourth or fifth lesson (talk) which made her want to call it love, attention to where it went with other things.

However low the sound of abstraction, the tone on the side of the ear being I had thought the letter that brings us back to where we were, fascinated and contemporary, as the cadence of this.

Not that they didn't have to be actually present, meaning a "ghost" is difficult to think of directly, separation like the sound of something happening in the same letter (later) amplified to be pleased by.

Avoiding what is difficult more than the feeling of talk or a pleasure she said I want, the man beginning slowly to sleep who happened to be young, whereas from that distance there are no answers.

What then it seems we are getting at, the feeling of elevation that continues after the fourth part somewhere else (more slowly) being suddenly the pleasure of sleep, only more so.

Originally somewhere else, more and more the talk which will continue to be a pleasure one would like, when suddenly I am at the beginning of the feeling of pleasure (slowly) getting nowhere.

That thought is a single method, anyone with whom I could sit for any length of time (think) or listen to the sound of *Moon* "read" in the two- or twelve-tone structure of music whose time you imagine you will miss.

Someone recording what I know about nothing, because I live in Kansas and when I leave it is gone, a repetition at any moment (since) bound to be breathtakingly simpler than what is.

Simpler that is than what enables us to act, how uncertain it is especially from a window, traveling as a present form (one) that music is measured by as a memory of this.

Or the form of what happens figured out, that one may return to Kansas (home) which is like the second or third part in a rhythmic structure whose units we are resigned to, divided, approximate.

II. "Composition as Process"

("Changes")

In the section beginning with sound (idea) parts determined to be used again precisely, this method affected by the present action of the body opposed by what appears to be possible.

What happens either to sound (intention) divided in the original series or events established in the listener's ear as a means of separating this phenomenon, as punctuation for instance measures differences between sounds, also more or less approximate.

One who increases the interval simply by walking toward what he felt, sound in other cases multiplied by the addition first of *Piano and Orchestra,* then of players analogous to shells on a beach.

Something described horizontally (apparent) as a means of arranging original events, this play of materials determined as an *Imaginary Landscape* whose absence will be read as an attempt at speech.

This situation characteristic of sound which means to depart from what is practical, the smallest parts (elements) necessary as *Variations,* exactitude of measurement occurring at discrete points on a line parallel to one's position with respect to another.

It being said that action is less a matter of beginnings and endings than the object, evident as notes in space suggest, conceived as the effect of sound on the radio or the experience of weather in precisely that place.

The experience of the man whose reply is immediate: "I remember talking in a line about a plane passing overhead, something in the distance like a question standing up, meaning that because you are the subject you have lost a friend."

Which one is thinking in *Music, Numbers* in pencil eliminating "the end" written as the first step (improvised) in listening to what the other one is actually thinking, changes in the original answer composed in ink.

By which I mean the sound of logic chosen as a form of walking on a beach, this "method" (spontaneous) exactly measured in one, two, three or four parts, one of which could as well be based on "material" namely of the heart.

In terms of this action the body known, *Interlude* opposed to a duration of potentially continuous moments written as a series of numbers which became in the final example indeterminate, as the line between one hand and the other disappeared.

This view for instance of extraordinary architecture characterized by its silence, *Construction* therefore subsequent to the material of sound itself, the listener who has entered into this act in relationship to the player walking into the opposite room.

One who knows that one is repeating actual sounds *in Metal, Sixteen* for instance the number of sounds used to compose the background, a situation one counted on discovered in analysis to be comparable to differences in frequency, timbre, and taste.

Whether one is satisfied by a given line (character) consciously or not, this play of *Changes* balanced by the subject described in comparable notation, the absence of the vertical line affirmed by examining its structure inside of that event.

Placing these five lines in order of their sounds, *Concert* meaning that what is left at intervals perpendicular to that movement holds for the following example, the remainder of the physical square (half) equal to the person left in the room.

Some duration of sound suggesting space, circumstance or the action of players in a history play, one voice (indicated) as it approaches the object on a page therefore read from the left, attention turned from the ear alone to what the person no longer present interrupts.

"That is not the story," standing either to ignore its desire or walk the other way, the second question "explainable" in one of three ways as a function of distance, the man "elevated" on a hill meaning he could come as close to never having raised his voice.

The other man writing notes in pencil: the other end of *Music* made in exactly the same way by listening to what it is, the instrument one almost becomes in thinking difference changes in the course of playing it, what he is doing (means) composed of notes.

("Indeterminancy")

The continuity of being given parts for example, bringing the character who is also determined to express in performance the possibility of material form, which is to say a method of notes with respect to *X*.

Or someone feeling at the point of "sleep" given the color of an outward reference (pertinent) at that point to a table of numbers following that event, the subject in either case comparable to his perception of interest in that.

X that is to say provided other elements in the work bring about its function, which by doing something arbitrarily may be controlled by structure (analysis) as the perception of numbers organized in the following way.

The object possessed by the character (material) who wishes to act conventional, where the presence of a beginning, middle, and end affect the performer who dictates his feelings (method) which is to say where the beat will be led to its climax.

The form of the body single in this case, enabling it to be attached to the situation of music on paper, *x* as it might have been printed at several points in the work performed in an unforeseen sense, stretched or unusually flat.

The situation of a building no matter when or what, being of course part of the sound of its content, the architect identified with respect to a procedure that repeats the object *Music* (thought) *Changes* specifically at the center of its act.

Intersection characteristic of the composer's range of control equally indeterminate, given that the performer in the play may be viewed as driving "boxes" of sound in a green light designated by the piano whose amplitude limits its use.

How the photographer may be his own subject, arbitrarily constructing the picture to follow his perception of an object the camera feels (analysis) going to "sleep," conscious of the probability that he may not be doing that.

One who is sound asleep identifying the father, his answer interpreted in a statement comparable to action no matter what, his knowledge of each performer composed as a mental event whose fluency is sometimes conscious, sometimes thought.

The relation of the instrument to its player for example on the table, the work itself moving from the architect's blueprint to the building (material) whose structure will be identified from that point of view.

This performance limited by being written, the performer himself expressive of certain practices in the tradition whose elements prohibit continuity, something he himself may bring to its material content.

The man described by the example of his feelings, sound that is to say (bias) like elements on the table equal to the person who suggests these sounds according to the presence of certain random theories of order.

The vertical position of the players involved in relation to the continuity of the silence between them, rectangles in a two-dimensional performance (system) removed for that reason in order to add its length to its width.

What is being seen from the side (consciously) no matter what the obstruction, the composer on the other hand knowing that each event penetrates the inversion of a different event seen from an opposite point of view.

Systems extending the performer's original function into parts whose continuity is indeterminate, a drawing of the head supplied to indicate the frequency of something (degree) characteristic of that morphology, division, or number of lines.

The subject himself acknowledged, his feeling opposite to an adjacent system arbitrarily viewed from the side (architecture) following the length of its inversion organized in terms related to its absence.

What that event becomes fixed in relation to its parts, a cubist painting of an object perhaps or picture analogous to the flicker it makes (purposeless) moving as an absence no matter what the score.

Likewise the object itself following its source, the amplitude of the shift in a relationship (inversion) more than what is present in each element for example, as the outcome of action in contrast to itself.

One action irrelevant with respect to the other, interior in that his response (frequency) includes material silence, a gamut of limitations (vision) of particular length, the performance of an available ending.

"Thought" itself calling the performer subject, a comparable change in direction announced as an interruption (meanwhile) of things approximate to events he prepares to notice by attaching himself to what he leaves.

Being like a performance of an object, where the outcome of action is not repeated as something other than seen, the knowledge that it happened recorded in a second postcard, grasped like land or air.

This sound spoken in the situation of a room in which the other person is essential to physical space itself, its architecture therefore an object which includes the separation of an audience into its parts.

All of this possible as music, the players (two) who recognize the sound of the second hand rising as if to depart, a suggestion on the radio that the performance of action will be different, variable, astonishing.

("Communication")

What if the question happens in time, two sounds in four-part harmony meaning one counts on something that is passing, the body going forward in order to ask what it is you want to say.

Intersection for instance at this moment, monotonous in the sense that each sound plays itself sometime (thinking) in a separate room, one of us changing direction sooner than the other.

Simply to say one is going back, purposeless as the telephone ringing or the effect of light in a glass of water (opposed) penetrated by seeing it as an actual thing, thinking one is causing that.

Analysis as I say when it "should" be letting go of components (variable) related by their failure to agree, like fingers one says fumbling in the dark at the frequency of the signal *near the end.*

What is actually meant by thinking one is at the center, what you say "again" letting go of the difference between each thought (independent) and a physical act, why the idea of the first performance wasn't right.

How memory could be itself something to hear when he wasn't looking, another body situated on the side of the theater unable to listen to measurable phenomena, the sound of a plane in the middle of the mouth.

Then asking "music" who has nothing to say, someone nearer to the sound of an interval (word) in the nervous system of the first one related to a second sound on the radio, appropriate enough to be performed.

Q whether it's active or not, applied as a method (music) opposite to an acoustic action which opens the ear "taking a nap," silence experienced as the difference between this circle and a continuum of points.

Parts of this drama analogous to the physical presence of the audience, intermediate nevertheless, diminished in notation as a representative of itself (author) imagined as points on the graph performed in light.

Which "voices" may begin to touch, the nostalgia of a character continuous with his motion at a particular distance *X,* the margin for example indicating that he has come from somewhere (pitch) circular.

Monotony more subjective than this, *finished* forms of motion said to be static, "global" in the sense that a sequence of parts may be expressed by doing nothing simultaneously, emphasis on itself.

Neglect in doing that of hearing and sight, the influence of a method continued to its position at the root of "things," harmony transformed to imitate a collision of elements passing like birds in the night.

"What" then of leaving, the subject turning in an opposite direction (range) beginning to walk away, that impulse at night for example neutralized by the position of the body on the ground, doing nothing.

People in a truck passing outside, the sound of the one you know but can't hear in *quotation* (audience) looking at something else, what has happened somewhere if the sound is not in words but people going.

How if we are going forward we know how to stop, count backwards, ask about the rhythm of water with respect to how it drops about my head, hearing instead of physics the question I would ask.

Something about the "tongue" (thinking) temporarily changing in another room, people one doesn't know slowing down to talk about getting sleepy, her experience "real" in that nothing happens, period.

Thought frequently produced in the same way, talking on the telephone (contemporary) instead of asking something else in writing that is to say, this "last" story separate from what is actually happening.

The temperature in the room adding to this difference, disorder in effect emphasized by "something" in another direction (variable) second to that, thinking that one walks away without having something to say.

Twelve tones in a series, the sound of writing itself situated in the body (going) say when you go to sleep, what happens after he opens his mouth measurable as the sound passing in a softer ear.

Why in the middle of physical activity the performance starts, which one of us says is going to sleep automatically, the other potential namely an impulse (less) to say something more than two *pianos.*

What "music" is appropriate whether it's performed in agreement with the second one, serious enough to ask if someone is nearer to the first one, vibrations related by an interval in the middle of that.

Sound then thinking in his own mind, a question of light waves seen before he *asked* to have it performed in his imagination (broadcast) I repeat, music representative of a circle known as zero.

The graph at another point distance notes equivalent to itself, admittedly present in performance as an acoustic experience *one is told,* intermediate as syntax or "taking a nap" speaking of that experience.

The same part touched (possible) in a continuous succession of lines, simultaneous in that nothing is performed in the collision between sound in the margin and the mind "voices" speak in an opposite direction.

III. "Lecture on Something"

Something about everything changing, the man on the bus who has nothing to say opposed to someone *on paper, the atmosphere* on one side of the *Intersection* changed by what seemed to be going on it "it."

It being separate, "contemplative" when he says what will happen when he comes to the object of that passage, the sound of the body precisely at rest, etc. rather than the shape of its desire.

Someone whose "form will appear," like the sound of an echo after it has happened or light on the mountain suddenly gone, the consequence of its shadows different than the object that makes it.

Otherwise continuity, as Hamlet means to accept the consequence of what happens no matter what, the one being killed (spirit) suggesting the musical terms for harmony, counterpoint, rhythm.

What the character in this situation chooses to say, meaning he isn't acting diminished, something about the duration of what happens at night answered by its relation to a permissible note.

The moment he is coming to rest, separate as an object turned on itself or elevated at the beginning of an opposite idea, this interruption (music) artificial in the sense that he is speaking it.

"That" said (talking) to be the difference between the first sound and its performance by someone else, who isn't actually pregnant but rather listening to the condition of the impulse to hear it.

Going rather to happen, this action in reference to something the foot continues to turn when the telephone rings, "silence" a consequence of the idea of memory familiar as the way a table works.

How something doesn't stop, the window one forgot at the beginning of a structure whose middle is occupied by other shoulders, speaking of a number it isn't possible to accept.

Out of that thinking the man is separate (clearly) from what happens, the effect of other action he doesn't observe regardless of his feeling, the nervousness of continuity in another movie.

Before that the picture of movement in space, the one pointing to the obstacle (disappearing) read as a condition of something equal to "it," the fact of its difference not to be only confused.

"See" for instance the way an event happens to the performer, the telephone he is going to answer (nothing) shifting to the sound of talk in the section on counterpoint, meaning continual.

This situation following in place of the right foot (something) "going down," the way she puts it as far as possible not to think "too much," emphatic as the painter who invades the place he paints.

On the other side of the first *section,* its limits changing the one who signs "it" above the work, *nothing (equal)* to the consequence he speaks as music seems to become the composer who is making it.

"Tranquil" suggesting the mountain at that point, the form it takes in contemplation of itself written as a footnote, disordered, which diminishes the area of silence associated with that event.

Haiku like that, less than the effect of light or sound on someone who makes it, saying it is also an illusion perhaps, how its form may be pleasing the moment he wakes regardless of the book.

No sound paradoxically at the opposite window, the other man who means (exception) what he says a possible idea, the one murdered at the door who vanishes at the end of the penultimate sentence.

These actions essentially out of character, as someone noted, beginning with what is acceptable to the one who chooses to explain it, being able to separate what simply happens from what it seems to resemble.

Falling light in an irrelevant view, thought itself interrupted in the middle of walking to the object (again) conclusively, the idea called *section* without continuity meaning it exists.

Someone possible at home "extraneous," the sound of that condition direct as something stopping silence, listening to the noise a word makes or "music" played on a piano extinguished by that.

"What" about action, as someone said, the piece before it difficult to conceive of, being as it turns out impossible to continue, imagine, say that it doesn't happen when it almost does.

How many windows and doors, speaking of the rhythm of music itself, which is to say a number one doesn't read, how it comes for example in writing to mean the beginning or possibility of talk.

No action observed as an effect of what happens then, two people at the piano eating an orange or feeling each other's activity as a separate thing, confident except that the man is thinking that.

"That is" (against) something, the idea of a work attached to saying it in a book read by others, philosophy or history or something about the nature of music equal to its movement (upwards) into air.

Mostly that something is abstract thought, how sculpture for instance can be referred to by the performer (incident) shifting in the last section to musical "time," generating nothing after that.

Out of this "escape" (that is) conclusion, how the tonic follows the dominant whether she keeps it going or not, something he said about the principle of a letter coming back to the same (made) place.

Writing/ Re: Memory

I.

> Some painters, including myself do not care what chair they are sitting on. It does not even have to be a comfortable one. They are too nervous to find out where they ought to sit. They do not want to "sit in style." Rather, they have found that painting—any kind of painting, any style of painting—to be painting at all, in fact—is a way of living today, a style of living so to speak. That is where the form of it lies.
>
> —Willem de Kooning, "What Abstract Art Means to Me"

What takes place between a writer and reader when language—a shared, referential, essentially public medium—informs subjective, essentially private experience? How can you know what I am thinking, feeling, and/or sensing when you live in another skin in a house far from here? By what dynamics does that most distant and abstract of relationships, the one between writer and reader, become not only possible but potentially intimate? How can words convey the world?

From its opening line—*Can one take captives by writing*— and in each sentence thereafter clear to the end, Lyn Hejinian's *The Guard* challenges us to ask questions such as these, questions variously aimed at discovering how any work of art mediates between artist and audience. Its premises are (1) that each of us experiences the world from a singularly unique point of view—a private eye, so to speak, whose frame of reference is shaped by the mixture of circumstance and psychological pressure that determines who and what we are; and (2) that language, though its conventions operate whenever language is used, requires what George Lakoff calls "the active participation of readers in the creation of meaning."[1] That is to say, the private world embodied in a writer's work becomes realized only when it is taken over—repossessed—by the co-operative, fully engaged reader. As Stevens put it, "The house was quiet and the world was calm. The reader became the book.[2]

Hejinian's work forces us to re-examine what it means to read a text. It invites us to step forward as participants, as necessary to the completion of the work as Hejinian herself was in writing it, by means of constant and disarmingly sudden shifts in syntax and substance, shifts of focus and ideas and direction that take place from sentence to sentence and within sentences, resulting in a multiplicity of separate parts whose interconnections (insistent but insistently not spelled out) will become articulate only to the reader who engages the text—the reader who in effect writes the poem each time he or she reads it.

As demanding as it is rewarding, this sort of engagement of an audience by the work of art is something like the one that came about in response to certain abstract expressionist paintings in the late 1940s and early 1950s. In the ambiguity of surface and depth in de Kooning's black and white *Painting* (1948), the astonishing network of poured lines and spatters in Pollock's *One (Number 31, 1950),* and the counterpoint of rough black grids on a white ground in Kline's *Painting Number 2* (1954), the three-dimensional world was not "represented" as in various ways it had been, from the cave paintings of Lascaux to Vermeer's domestic interiors to Picasso's *Les Demoiselles d'Avignon.* Rather, these works make the viewer stop, literally stop, just at the edge of the canvas, simply because there is no recognizable person or scene depicted there, no illusion of the world upon which to focus. Denied the comfort of narrative content, the viewer is forced to direct full attention toward the lines and shades and tones of color that make up the canvas plane. At the same time, because a work like de Kooning's *Painting* is informed by an almost frenetic activity of shapes and lines and textures, we are moved to ask, What is the relation of this line to that, that shape to this, this area to that? We are invited to figure out the work by becoming intimately and actively involved with its raw material—paint.

The Guard makes similar demands on a reader's attention, the terms of which may be described in some detail. Take the opening verse paragraph of part 1:

> *Can one take captives by writing—*
> *"Humans repeat themselves."*
> *The full moon falls on the first. I*
> *"whatever interrupts." Weather and air*
> *drawn to us. The open mouths of people*
> *are yellow & red—of pupils.*
> *Cannot be taught and therefore cannot be.*
> *As a political leading article would offer*
> *to its illustrator. But they don't invent*
> *they trace. You match your chair.*

Though its syntax indicates that line 1 is a question, the lack of appropriate punctuation at the end of the line ("—" instead of "?") together with the indicative statement that follows immediately upsets our expectations: not only do we not get an answer to the question, we don't get the question. And yet, *Can one take captives by writing—* does make sense as a question, albeit one whose terms themselves demand clarification: how "take captives" (by possession of the ear? mind?), which "captives" (readers?), how "by writing" (words in print? in the air?)? The question is thus perceived as being at once syntactically complete and semantically wide open. Having committed herself to words in print, the poet's ideas are at this point out in the world, available like a loose ball at center court to be taken up and carried forward by any reader capable of an equal commitment.

The most obvious way of understanding line 2, *"Humans repeat themselves."* is as an answer to the posed yet open-ended question that precedes it. But does the indicative statement, whose echoes reach back at least to Herodotus's warning that those who do not understand history are doomed to repeat it, constitute a "yes" or "no" answer to that question? One assumes the truth of *"Humans repeat themselves"* to be incontrovertible, but in what sense exactly does Hejinian mean for us to take the pronouncement: why is line 2 in quotations? Are these "Humans" the same "captives" that "writing" can (or cannot) "take" by virtue of the fact that they are characteristically given to "repeat themselves?" In fact, though their proximity suggests a close logical relation between lines 1 and 2, there is a rather huge disjunction that informs the poem's opening sentence. The reader who would activate this text finds him- or herself as if on an iceflow, where to negotiate the crevasses that abruptly divide one statement from the next requires as much agility and courage, the willingness to leap, as Hejinian must have had when she crossed here.

Line 3, *The full moon falls on the first,* seems in some ways to stand in distinct opposition to line 2. Where that line focused our attention upon mankind, we are now asked to consider "nature," represented by means of a synecdoche as the full moon that, instead of rising, as one might expect in the rhetoric of description, here "falls on the first"—day of the month?—if so, a location not so much in the physical heavens as a particular box on the calendar, that human invention made to keep track of time. And like those humans who do certain things again and again, the full moon here falls on the first just as it has periodically for thousands of years. We see then that nature repeats itself just as we do, an inference suggested by other means in the phonetic linkage between lines 2 and 3: the long *u*-vowel-*n* sounds in *Humans* and *moon,* the *s*-vowel-*l*-*f*/*v* sounds in *themselves* scrambled to *f*/*v*-vowel-*ls* sounds in *falls.*

Unlike the two preceding lines, line 3 is not complete at the end of its completed and completely unified (by sound as well as sense) syntactic unit: *The full moon falls on the first. I.* The first-person pronoun—or is it roman numeral *I,* a movement from "first" to "one" to "eye"?—stands here at once in contrast to the preceding subject (*moon*) and as a specific instance of the generalized subject of line 2 (*Humans*). And the straightforward, indeed commonplace, indicative statements of those two lines leads us to expect a similar, easy-to-assimilate predicate following the subject: *I/ "whatever interrupts."* Instead, *"whatever interrupts"* simultaneously interrupts the statement being made and defines it, precisely yet tautologically, in terms of itself. The quotation marks here echo those around line 2, but the sense of "interrupts" seems oddly out of joint with the suggestion of things being done over and over again contained in the word *repeat* and the regular recurrence of both full moon and first of month. And again, the reader is asked to supply connections that seem to be missing—for example, the absent but syntactically suggested verb that supplies transitive sense to whatever "interrupts" (*I/* [tolerate/expect/respond to/write down] *"whatever interrupts"*)—to fill the space left open by a shift even more startling than the ones we have encountered up to now. If we hadn't known before that this writing, *The Guard,* would demand our full and energetic attention, *I/ "whatever interrupts"* serves us notice: *en gard.*

What follows in line 4, *"whatever interrupts." Weather and air,* also doesn't follow, at least in substance, though the vowel-plus-r sounds in *whatever, interrupts, Weather* and *air* provides clear phonetic linkage between the two statements. The near phonetic identity of *whatever* and *Weather* indeed helps to make accessible their logical interconnection: weather is, after all, something that interrupts (the game was called in the bottom of the fourth because of rain, Yankees leading five to four), and weather is carried in the air. As the sentence unfolds, however, the verb again appears to be missing: *Weather and air/ drawn to us.* Thus, the reader is again urged to participate, in this instance to supply the link between subject and complement (can we miss hearing *are* in *air?*). But again, despite the relatively easy syntax here, there is again an abrupt substantive shift, in that the sense of something being "drawn to" (pulled toward) is nearly opposite that of "interrupts" (forcing things apart). This opposition seems to parallel another shift in sense, in that the syntax of Hejinian's apparent but never-quite-made assertion that *Weather and air* [are] *drawn to us* reverses the normal relation of agent-reagent in a world in which humans are attracted to and dependent upon the life-giving forces embodied in weather and air. In presenting an alternative point of view (nature is attracted to us), this statement invites the reader to rethink the whole tradition of anthropomorphism—man at the center of his cosmos, the stars and planets wheeling harmoniously about him—not as scientific fact but syntactic possibility. As such, it makes a major claim for language itself, for the power of words to shape our understanding of our experience in the world: "Ideas cross the landscape and become horizon and the weather."[3]

I want to talk for a moment about what happens in line 5 between the end of one sentence and the beginning of the next: *air/ drawn to us. The open mouths of people.* Surely there is a more than tenuous logical thread joining these two statements together, since *people,* the object of the preposition *of,* is a third person restatement of the first person indirect object, *us;* and people do in fact breathe (draw in) air through open mouths. At the same time, however, there is just as surely a tremendous gap between the partially complete semantic units in this line, a shift forced by the change in grammatical point of view (first-person to third) and an apparent abandoning of one subject (weather and air—forces in nature) for the next (open mouths—a part of the body). The fact that the poem's syntactic/logical units are radically discontinuous, its train of thought apparently derailed, makes powerful demands upon a reader used to narrative and/or ideational continuity, the sort of continuity that allows one to sit back and be led by the writer through a series of statements whose linkages are essentially straightforward. Because the connective tissue holding the pieces of *The Guard* together is most often oblique, literally transparent, the reader must work to bridge the gaps between one verse unit and the next: reader as much as writer composes the text. Hejinian's comments upon her aims and practice in a later work, *The Green,* are instructive:

> One of the results of this compositional technique, building a work out of discrete intact units (in fact, I would like each sentence itself to be as nearly a complete poem as possible), is the creation of sizeable gaps between the units. The reader (and I can say also the writer) must overleap the end stop, the period, and cover the distance to the next sentence. "Do not lovers of poetry," asks Keats, "like to have a little Region to wander in where they may pick and choose, and in which the images are so numerous that many are forgotten and found new in

a second reading. . . . Do not they like this better than what they can read before Mrs. Williams comes down the stairs?" [John Keats to Benjamin Bailey, October 8, 1817.] Meanwhile, what stays in the gaps, so to speak, remains crucial and informative. Part of the reading occurs as the recovery of information (looking behind) and the discovery of newly structured ideas (stepping forward).[4]

The predicate that follows *The open mouths of people/ are yellow and red—of pupils* at once provides us with the comfort of semantic closure (yes, open mouths can look yellow and red) and immediately upsets that sense by introducing a prepositional phrase, *of pupils,* which, because it rhymes phonetically and logically with the phrase *of people,* seems to qualify, or disqualify, our initial reading of line 5. Are we in fact talking about the mouths of *pupils*—a particular subclass of people—rather than about people in general? Or are these the eyes' pupils, therefore related not so much to *people* above as to *mouths?* The suggestion of a school in what follows offers one rationale for the shift from *people* to *pupils,* but the absence of an explicit subject in the sentence *Cannot be taught and therefore cannot be* (a perfectly regular line of iambic pentameter, and also the first line in which syntactic and verse-line closure coincide), coupled with the oddly askew reworking of the Cartesian proposition, make for a distinctly private hermeneutics, yet one that is presented in language whose matter of fact tone is not only accessible but literally public: students in schools cannot be taught.

As in one sense at least the period at the end of line 7 seems to bring a sentence without a subject to premature closure (*Cannot be taught and therefore cannot be . . .* what?—trusted? graduated? counted upon to become useful members of society?),[5] the sentence that follows in lines 8 and 9 is joined to what precedes it by certain frames of reference, though it too remains syntactically incomplete. That is, *As a political leading article would offer/ to its illustrator* acts like a dependent clause whose sponsor forgot to show up and who therefore moves to attach itself to whatever is nearest, in this instance, whatever *Cannot be taught and therefore cannot be.* Because that line established a context in which the classroom and what goes on in it is an immediate possibility, one makes a relatively easy leap to the following reference to *a political leading article* and *its illustrator,* both of which fit that context in several ways at once: political, therefore public; a leading article, as in a newspaper, which can be illustrated as in a political cartoon; or is this leading article grammatical, as in *The full moon* or *The open mouths,* which might not offer its illustrator much if any referentiality to draw upon.

While the meaning of the incomplete syntactic unit in lines 8 and 9 reaches back for fulfillment toward the similarly incomplete unit in line 7, it also reaches forward into the syntactically and semantically complete sentence that follows it in lines 9 and 10: *But they don't invent/ they trace.* The signal of a logical turn inherent in the conjunction *But* is comforting (at last, syntactic direction to tell us where we're going) but also tantalizingly oblique—what fact is about to be contradicted? which turn is being made? The pronoun references are equally demanding of the reader's active engagement: does *they* refer to *illustrator*(s), *article*(s), *pupils, people, Humans?* One means of illustration, of course, is to lay a transparent sheet of paper over the page and "trace" what shows through, as in the root sense of the Latin, *trahare,* to draw (compare *drawn* in line 5). But, as the stanzaic unit moves toward completion, the dynamics in *But they don't invent/ they trace* are far more complicated than this. For *trace* can also suggest "to follow," as in tracing footprints, which causes it to stand both in opposition to the idea introduced in *leading* and at the same time in conjunction with the ideas clustered variously in *repeat* (line 2), *drawn to us* (5), *Cannot be taught* (7—compare the root meaning of *educate,* to draw out), and, though we haven't yet come to it, *match* (11). These multiple senses of *trace* as drawing and following all stand in contrast to the sense of the preceding verb, *invent,* also from a Latin root meaning to come in or to, that is, to discover (*I/ "whatever interrupts"*). Incidentally, it may be worth noting that the highly energized, disparate effects by which the sentence *But they don't invent/ they trace* is attracted to and opposed by other elements within the stanza are casually downplayed—de-emphasized, as it were, to become "mere" unnoticed effects calling little or no attention to themselves, and by that token all the more powerful—by the concentrated phonetic patterning in long *a* and *nt* sounds, which work to unify the sentence itself and so to isolate it, at least phonetically, from the sentences that precede and follow it, sentences in which the long *a* and *nt* sounds do not occur.

I have already mentioned that the idea suggested by *match* in *You match your chair* echoes ideas that have been running throughout the stanza. The shift in pronouns from third to second person in this line *(they/You)* is contradicted by the ideational similarity of *trace* and *match,* both of which have to do with something fitting or copying something else. One literally matches one's chair in that the shaped contours of the wooden or plastic seat mold one's posterior when one sits (an overstuffed living room chair is likewise molded by the shape that sits in it): the form of one object "matches"—fits, corresponds to, informs—that of the other. The first object here, however, is not merely a thing but *you,* the reader, and by extension the writer who finds words to shape her experience in the world. The writer matches her "chair" (does one hear the Latin root *cathedra,* from which cathedral, and/or echoes of the French *chère,* flesh?) in that her words attempt to inform—literally to remember—a world that is too large and various, too shifting, ever to be fixed in words on a page. And yet the possibility that words may be made into world continues to take hold and possess us, for as Hejinian puts it, "the incapacity of language to match the world permits us to distinguish our ideas and ourselves from the world and things in it from each other."[6] In writing the world, the writer delineates herself in relation to it:

The landscape is a moment of time
that has gotten in position.

My familiar home is thickset.

Passages in italics are from *The Guard* (Berkeley: Tuumba, 1984; reprinted in *The Cold of Poetry* [Los Angeles: Sun & Moon Press, 1994]).

II.

How then can words "write" the world, construct the writer's experience of it, her perception of the moment whose moment passes even before she knows it? Not simply by describing, as Stein discovered ("the words or words that made what I looked at *be* itself [my italics] . . . had as I say nothing whatever to do with what any words would do that described that thing"[7]), but by creating in words an articulation of the world that words themselves sound (echo) and shape.

The target of such writing is literally to "remember" the world, to construct in language what Hejinian has called *the disquieting runs of life.*[8] Its premise is that writing, if it can bear intently enough upon the data perceived in the passing moment, can grasp/make present that moment as an equivalence, a created "remembered" form in language, writing as the physical embodiment, in words, of world. As Stein discovered, the objective of such writing has nothing whatever to do with description. But whereas Stein in *Tender Buttons* focused on *things*—objects, food, rooms—which she found more possible to get hold of in words than people (because umbrellas, feathers, teacups, and red hats do not move, whereas people do), Hejinian in *Writing Is an Aid to Memory* aims to catch hold of whatever *disquieting runs of life* arrive, slip by. The point isn't to "record" what happened last Sunday—lunch with good friends in a field full of spring wildflowers—because to reconstitute that scene and that experience as "description" mixed with narrative will interpose language and its structures between Hejinian (and thence her readers) and her life. Rather, the point is to make language itself *be* the writer's experience in and of the world.

Writing is an aid to memory because it *articulates* ("sounds" and "shapes") memory—not only gripping the past in words ("What memory is not a gripping thought," as Hejinian writes in *My Life*) but making present ("spelling") experience in words—*other* experience, analogue to, echo of the experience out of which writing itself grows. Memory takes place as an articulation in, by, and of writing because "[Memory—I am *misquoting* Wittgenstein here] is not *translated* into words when it is expressed. The words are not a translation of something else when it is expressed. The words are not a translation of [memory] that was there before they were."[9] Words are the material form of memory, rather, the sound and also shape of its physical embodiment, which doesn't so much represent what takes place in memory as it literally "remembers" those remembered events, *as words.* Inseparable from events in words, events in thought/memory are thus "spelled" in—by means of—writing itself. Language, the phenomenon as such, is in this sense the element of memory/thought: "What memory is not a gripping [word]?" which suggests the actual physics by which events in words "grasp" events in the world. "The obvious analogy is with with music," as Hejinian writes elsewhere in *My Life,* which calls to mind Zukofsky's sense of connection between the structures in music (and, I would add, words) and the world: "Materialist philosophers of history may do well to think about Bach's remark: The order which rules music is the same order that controls the placing of stars and the feathers in a bird's wing."[10]

Consider the opening section of *Writing Is an Aid to Memory:*

apple is shot nod
ness seen know it around saying
think for a hundred years
but and perhaps utter errors direct the point to a meadow
rank fissure up on the pit
arts are several branches of life
little more science is brought where great
need is required
out becomes a bridge of that name
in the painting is a great improvement
bit ink up on the human race
and return if the foot goes back
in the trunks of trees behoove a living thing
wedge war common saw
hard by that length of time the great demand is
very dear
ashes in water
that might be a slip of architecture
think was reduced to an improper size
blocks to interest who can visit
variations on ideas are now full
problems
from a point of increasing
at only as to four or we who nine
a little grace familiar with simple limbs and the sudden
reverse.

apple is shot nod opens as if in the middle of a sentence whose beginning we have not been witness to: which apple? where? why? how? Then a sudden gleam of sense: *apple is shot* may suggest a context we do know, can remember: William Tell and his son; or does *shot* mean what it means on the street, "finished," "done for." In other words, our experience of the poem's first three words enacts in a fraction of an instant something quite like what it is to be faced with the incremental detail of our experience in the world: at any given moment we simultaneously take in new information, connect it to what we already know, anticipate where it's going. What comes next here, *nod,* produces immediate vertigo. Whatever frame of reference *apple is shot* may have started to fit into suddenly begins to slip away. *nod* is related to *shot* by sound, of course, and by suggesting a motion of the head may also continue to suggest William Tell's son's head—as the arrow flies toward it? immediately as the apple is struck? just after, as sign of, yes, a good shot?

That my attempted reading of this line may, though it makes sense, have nothing whatever to do with what Hejinian had in mind suggests something important about her writing practice throughout *Writing Is an Aid to Memory.* Putting words together into contiguous relationships that, like *the disquieting runs of life* she speaks of in the book's preface, keep *slipping by,* she makes the raw material of life literally present: as language, the data of the world translated say into words that, as we read them, we try to make coherent sense of, find the *message* in. But as in one's experience of everyday reality, that message is oblique, opposed to us, open to revaluation as one's point in time or position in the landscape changes. So that every answer, conclusion, observation, judgment, insight is at best provisional, subject to change at a moment's notice, indeed without notice—emotional response also thus provisional, ranging from possible delight to deep disquiet to indifference, depending on one's mood.

The precipitous shift from *nod/ ness seen know it around saying* upsets whatever temporary equilibrium a reader may have determined for herself to this point. Whereas the passage opened with a recognizable, albeit incomplete, syntax (*apple is shot* = subject-verb-complement), the string of monosyllables beginning to sound (*shot nod/ ness seen know*) seems to take part in no familiar grammatical structure or pattern of meaning. *ness* by itself at the start of the line appears to be attached as a suffix to a word now missing from the end of the previous line ("holi-," "blind-," etc.). The physical spacing of lines on the page, where each line starts at the position of the letter in the alphabet stretched across the page (hence the "a" of "apple" at left margin), suggests to the eye the possibility that the entire poem is itself a fragment, a ruin, part of what had been in some prior, more perfect state a completed thing, the whole poem: the poem is always itself potentially missing, left out, its text fragmentary by procedural definition; as readers we find ourselves faced with what amounts to a portion of the whole, which now no longer exists, this being only what can be at this time remembered of it. In a sense, then, our experience of Hejinian's poem is not unlike our experience of the Parthenon, the Venus de Milo, or the tapestries that hang in the Cloisters in New York, works the absence of whose former state—which we can only imagine, and which in our imagination must be more nearly perfect, more ideal, than the fraction that remains—challenges us to recreate the whole from its part, invites us to become artists as audience.

In any case, given that what we see on the page is all there is, *nod/ ness seen* makes no clear sense. At the same time, hints of possible lines of connection ([Loch] ness [monster] seen? seen nodding? *ness* an orthographic near-scrambling of *seen?*) persuades us that there is a sense to be found here, a message to be determined, meaning to be created in the mind of the reader who engages this text fully as far as Hejinian herself did in writing it. And quite apart from serpents swimming in Scottish lakes, the verbal sequence mapped out in *seen know it around saying* puts before us, as if compressed in a small hard shell, just that series of operations Hejinian as poet, and all of us as humans, undertake as we take in and attempt to articulate any given aspect of our experience. Words here engage present tense immediately, without syntactic cement; the effect is one of wonderfully bright, clear, sudden freedom—of all Hejinian's works, this book particularly possessed of youthful intellectual delight, the full range of mind's potential grasped and held an instant, or more, all that can be known around saying.

think for a hundred years goes both forward and backward in at least two ways at once. It moves the poem forward literally, as the verse line proceeds, and ideationally, as one person's saying becomes another's (a listener's) thinking about what has been said, now and perhaps into the future, for a hundred years to come. (*think for a hun-*

dred years may also stand grammatically as the object of *saying,* i.e., as if in quotation marks, what is to be said.) But it also moves the poem back, the idea of *think*[ing] an echo of *know* in the line before, and the time span *a hundred years* as equally past as yet to come, in any event a far larger frame than the *see/know/say* which precedes it.

If one takes *think for a hundred years* as the object of that all but instantaneous cluster, *but and perhaps utter errors direct the point to a meadow* starts at least to continue that direction of thought: *think for a hundred years/ but . . . .* What follows at once interrupts the about-to-be-made contrary statement suggested by *but* (notice, though, that *and* is linked grammatically to *but:* both are conjunctions) and, with a telling shift in perspective introduced—almost as if an afterthought—by the suggestion of pure uncertainty in *perhaps,* carries forward a number of verbal threads: *utter* and *direct* as imperative verbs aligned with *think; utter* an echo of *saying; the point* perhaps the one that shot the apple, which grows on a tree in a meadow. Nor in this poem is this reading exhaustive, for it makes equally good sense to take *utter* as an adjective modifying those *errors* that themselves *direct* some *point* (intellectual rather than physical, as the point of that story) to a place in the landscape, or, from another perspective, to take *point* as a verb ideationally akin to *saying, utter,* and *direct,* which in effect cuts off the object about to be named in the statement *direct the / point.*

The potential vertigo induced in a reader by the simultaneity of literal "events" I am describing here—and failing to describe since they take place in only the time it takes to print these words on the brain's screen—is the kind of feeling one might have every day, faced with the even greater multiplicity of detail one takes in from moment to moment, were it not for the mind's ability to focus and select. Life's data, what Hejinian calls in her preface *raw confusions,* being incessant, continuous in at least four dimensions until (one's) life ends, this writer's challenge is to demonstrate, by reenactment, the simple truth *that truth cannot end.*

> *Continuous quantities, like continuous qualities, are endless like the truth, for it is impossible to carry them. It is impossible to carry light and darkness, proximity, chance, movement, restlessness, and thought. From all of these, something spills.*

What *spills* out of the meadow, *rank fissure up on the pit,* condenses the oppositions inherent in paradox into several nodes. To begin with *rank,* whose sense as noun (a row, line, an orderly arrangement) absolutely contradicts its sense as adjective (overly luxuriant, grown to excess), and whose sense as transitive verb (to place in a rank or ranks) collapses as soon as it is coupled to the idea contained in *fissure* (a division along a line). The linearity suggested in *fissure* is itself collapsed, or rather, as perspective shifts, closes down from line to the single, round, open hollow placed suddenly before us in *pit,* which just as suddenly reverses the literal climb begun in the line's prepositional construction, *up on.* (Notice the echo of an identical construction seven lines later, in *bit ink up on the human race,* which despite an array of grammatical possibilities—*bit* as noun or verb, *ink* as noun or verb—similar to the ones outlined here, has nothing else whatever to do with *fissure up on the pit.* But that is, as they say, another story.)

Not to make molehills out of prepositions, but the idea of height suggested in *up on* (and simultaneously, and more insistently, contradicted in *fissure* and *pit*) *is* carried over into *arts are several branches of life,* where the word *branches* invites us to think not only of branches high up in a tree—the tree of life, other of whose features appear later (*trunks of trees, limbs*)—but of lines, divisions in a system of classification, therefore of *rank* and, from another point of view, *fissure.* And while it is indeed true that *the arts are several branches of life*—along with other human endeavors such as, say, the sciences or economics—the verbal information we pick up as the line unfolds demonstrates in little, by coincidental echoes of and allusions to information from before, that this art, poetry, can be made to *be* life. *arts are,* for example, a thought complete with intransitive verb, repeats with variation the sound pattern heard in *shot nod* and, in a different way, *utter errors,* and the also momentarily complete statement *arts are several* (verb now transitive, message changed into tautology) echoes the syntax, sound, and sense of *apple is shot.* The root of *several* (to separate) in front of *branches,* contains the seed running through a whole series of words, from *rank* to *fissure* to *branches,* and itself counteracts the root meaning of *arts* (to join, fit together).

What Hejinian has articulated in *Writing Is an Aid to Memory*—fragments of perception, insight, sudden awareness of (literal) events operating in several systems of logic simultaneously—invites her reader in effect to "write" her text. The minute mental explosions her writing sets off (in us) take place to the extent that reader becomes writer: enters the text, sees what Hejinian in her preface calls the *sinews and bones* of a language she is given *the power to say different things at one time with or without different parts, of view, exploring what has been a mind, unknown.* What goes on as the poem goes forward is more of the same, each point alive with multiple possibilities, each charged particle set to go off soon as the reader releases it:

arts are several branches of life
little more science is brought where great
need is required
out becomes a bridge of that name
in the painting is a great improvement
bit ink up on the human race
and return if the foot goes back
in the trunks of trees behoove a living thing
wedge war common saw
hard by that length of time the great demand is
very dear
ashes in water
that might be a slip of architecture
think was reduced to an improper size
blocks to interest who can visit
variations on ideas are now full
problems
from a point of increasing
at only as to four or we who nine
a little grace familiar with simple limbs and the sudden
reverse.

And so on, and on, through 42 such sections—like riding three or four horses at once ("impossible" on horseback but possible here), writing is an aid to memory, Hejinian's memory, for one thing, of her life as it takes place, *a little grace familiar with simple limbs and the sudden / reverse.* Her reader's memory as well, whose thought wakes to the alarm clock the words sound, calling us forward to the *incessant knowledge*—certain, uncertain, but wholly generous in its endeavor to make present all that might be found out of this time and place—we give to the poem the poet gives to us:

> *The trees of the street are laid down. A bedroom is cut where I went. Where I mean to will have to come to me. Though we keep company with cats and dogs, all thoughtful people are impatient, with a restlessness made inevitable by language.*

Passages in italics are from *Writing Is an Aid to Memory* (Great Barrington, MA: The Figures, 1978).

III. (*My Life*)

Within the fabric of the text of Lyn Hejinian's *My Life* the bits and pieces of past and present in lapidary imbrication, one upon the other in what order the words themselves would find, interweave. *Only fragments are accurate,* we read, followed by *Break it up into single words, charge them to combination.* Which points up another thread concurrent in *My Life* with the autobiography: namely, that set of proposals directed toward mapping an aesthetics of perception. For just as Hejinian questions the "accuracy" of writing the past as if the present didn't count—yesterday disembodied so to speak from today, history as if it could exist without someone to remember it—she feeds us *passim* an assortment of speculations focused upon both how a writing such as hers might be practiced and what its effects might be:

> *Such displacements alter illusion, which is all to the good*
> *Thinking about time in the book, it is really the time of your life*
> *What memory is not a "gripping" thought*
> *The obvious analogy is with music.*

Take this reading of section 21, simply proposed as demonstration of how the work works, both itself and upon us.

The epigraph to this section,

> *We are not*
> *forgetting the*
> *patience of the*
> *mad, their love of*
> *detail*

acts as a kind of floating voice part, which strikes us from some as yet unidentified region outside the frame of present discourse, here as elsewhere a retelling or foretelling of the text, one aim of whose patience and love of detail is not to forget (a practice of writing hardly mad, it would seem, even if they too be included).

> *The summer countryside with the round hills patchy and dry, reminding one of a yellow mongrel dog, was what one could call a dirty landscape, the hills colored by the dusty bare ground rather than by grass, and yet this is what seemed like real country to me.*

Straightforward, conventional in its prose rhythms, at least, the reference sharply focused as the dog (love of detail) perceived as dusty ground seems unqualified, direct as the arrow about to hit the target affixed in section 20 to the just baled hay. It is summer in a landscape one finds familiar whether or not one "knows" it in fact—"writing as an aid to [hypnosis]"? readers "take[n] captive" by text?

I had idealized the pioneer's life, sinking roots.

Familiar then as the idea of landscape those preceding us in time and space had crossed, recalling as well by echo the closing line of section 20: *Could the prairie be this sea—for love.* The reader knows it, the landscape that is, in the mind the words conjure—*My Life* so appealing because its words so convincing (again, text as hypnosis, seduction even)—the poet's life into which the lives of those before her *sinking roots* arrive, in that place

Known for its fleas.

—known at most now from books or from the movies.

One could touch the flesh of their secrets, the roses of their behavior.

Perhaps, if one had way sufficient enough to bring the fact of flesh to bear here, or touch the flower the young wife would nurture in the yard. It will bloom this spring, and the grass will turn green, and she will grow big with child.

One didn't know what to give a young woman.

As usual, there in Kansas or here in Oakland, what to give to whom in this case a reader's guess, the woman suddenly as much Hejinian at some point in her own life as any other one she might imagine. But not only is the question posed by this syntax Who receives the unsaid gift but Who gives it, which "one"? Likely as not a man, hers perhaps, what follows leading us to such a fact:

Watermen are such as row in boats.

Whereupon we leave the prairie for the sea or river—Lewis and Clark on the Missouri? poling up and rowing back?—rose buds for row boats bound for we don't know which port. Who's in charge here, one asks legitimately across the space between "woman" period "Watermen" whose hands and backs to the oars propels us, the reader, as if backward. But

> *They don't hear a word of all this, floating like plump birds along the shore.*

—out of earshot over the water, these words able nonetheless to picture them, or remember—"a 'gripp[ed]' thought."

> *In extending, then entangling their concerns, they are given a thousand new names.*

Each one as if a net cast out over the landscape (also the reader's "sensibility") language gains access to, opening territory the pioneers first thought best was theirs, enables the other to be named. From which social ills, small mind crowded, bent upon history repeats itself,

> *The lace curtain Irish hate neighborhood Blacks.*

Called to by name on the street between buildings, one turned around a split second.

> *The coffee drinkers answered ecstatically.*

—caffeine intensive or not at once the issue the words spell, stepping literally out of station. Given their reply, content of which unknown to us rejoins the as yet unposed question, or question posed in the movie next door, which runs concurrently to this one, wherein one might see, had one access, an alternate text of *My Life:*

> *We looked at the apartment and took it.*

The phonetic alignment of verbs, each of which establishes fixed relation between perceiver and object perceived (as "*see*" in Chinese is represented by an eye above legs, running through space), here places us squarely at home. Like the ones before us we move in, unpack, hang pictures, walk streets to find how

> *Space has small neighborhoods.*

Everything is new here, in this place and this book, around each corner the new sentence disclosing its complete surprise.

> *As for we who "love to be astonished," each new bit of knowledge is merely indicative of a wider ignorance.*

So what we think we know and/or remember may lead, does and will always take us, just to the edge of a circle of perceptions whose center I am, you are, converging. What we do with that fact of moments juxtaposed one to another in place of time, "the concept," is almost to be able to know where we are just as it passes into the forthcoming present. To write her life truly Hejinian believes, indeed proves, will be done. Other means considered but no.

> *One might cultivate a charming defect, say a romantic limp*
> *or a little squint.*

As indeed one does, once in a while, or did, whatever the terms of endearment. (Think of Byron and the nearsighted ones whose "charms" have persuaded us, rightly enough, these many years.) Now the terms though have changed, girl grown older, moved in with a man to a place below one window of which the printed sign reads "Apartment for Rent."

> *I made curtains out of colored burlap from Sears, hung them*
> *at the four windows of the green apartment.*

As simply as the event it remembers, language encoding for the reader who would take it up, *see* that room, eyes running on legs to be there, the words say what she saw, sewing, moving on.

> *Down manholes, through pipes, to the mysterious sea.*

The water then flowing from kitchen tap to where watermen, once again, could row through it. Confined spaces here, however, inside pipes layed under the street, where plumbing goes from all the houses on it; and in one of those she finds herself, the story goes, inhaling:

> *Though the pantry smelled more strongly of spices than of herbs*
> *and was dominated by nutmeg, the kitchen itself tended to smell of*
> *everything that had ever been cooked, but only because it was dark.*

Here then another "sinking roots," the person herself for one thing moving in, thinking plants from a field dried and stored in jars or plucked fresh from the garden.

> *If you cut your nails they will grow back thick, blunt, like a man's.*

So what then to be done with so much time on her hands, so little space, to say it say in thirty-seven sentences, but to recall contentment (born of all the time in the world to recall)—like Stein in *Lucy Church Amiably.*

> *In a little while, he said, we should be thumbing home.*

His thumb, no doubt, blunt as a man's, apartment now become the word we name the place we live in we hope by choice, arriving there by whatever means accessible. Hitch in this case hiking, thumb asking a ride the twentieth sentence,

There were five little kittens under the car.

suggests was forthcoming, though this one could like as not be any Ford or Chevrolet beneath whose chassis she once glimpsed them. Perhaps the time one drove for hours, far out into the country, the night one learned

They had put curves in the highway to keep drivers awake.

At other times the levels mix, surface charged as if to retain for itself the shifting of language into a realm we both do and don't keep up with:

> *The obvious analogy is with music, which extends beyond the space the figure occupies.*

Which figure, though, one asks, wondering is it the theme or phrase returning to the root or the person who plays same:

She was pumping her violin over the piano.

And where then is that, living room? concert hall?—and when—last night? years ago or more? And does the next sentence, following as if in a context we know we follow as well, offer answer?

> *Each evening before dinner my parents sat for a while in the "study," to talk, while my mother knit decoratively designed French sweaters called Jacquard.*

Domestic, then, tranquility, a life at home full of what one hears, indeed dreams, of being all that any of us might in a certain life want—in a sense at least, connections to follow, order at home reflecting order in the world beyond "study" walls:

The house sparrow is a weaver finch.

Therefore, thus as it were, that nature "herself" does what one's mother does, first in fact and second here, in words aligned to bring about perception of combined shifting planes the person beholds. Inside this house, outside the sparrow,

The front door key is hidden under the aloe.

So standing, as if on a porch, one picks up the plant and prepares to enter through this door, into that room, where those people talk and knit, the writer tells us, moving us in and out of the picture:

How did the artist think to put that on the outside.

—she asks, becoming herself both that one and the questioner, moving us about by making attention, click, then shift.

Such displacements alter illusions, which is all-to-the-good.

Which we have heard before in different context, chapter and verse; insistence, reiteration, the point then to draw out—educate—by example and demonstration how this mixing of past with continuous present writing the life writes *My Life.*

Now I too could find a perfect cantaloupe, not by poking at the
flesh around the stem of the melon but by sniffing at it.

Something one's mother, perhaps, teaches that one learns (*for my mother & my father*), an almost mystic coordination of senses in which one hands back along the line the information each perceives. This one is ripe, let me cut it, you see what I mean. . . . Until,

At some point hunger becomes sensuous, then lascivious.

—then so to eat will it quench thirst, satisfy desire, or shall we continue in this mode, call it foreplay,

Not a fuck but a hug.

—which precedes, and will prolong, intimate pleasure. This being not the sense one talks of in the "study," this being performed in other rooms of her house, or other house across the land at later time; or before—before, or after love had cooled.

My mother threw away all those little objects of sentiment,
billed foolishness.

Think of the walls of pictures, mementoes, the scrap and yearbook junior year, the girl then full of feeling. In that memory—"a 'gripping' thought"—she does an instant reside. But

The reference is a distraction, a name trimmed with colored ribbons.

Pretty, perhaps, indeed pretty, but one is here now and that is in the mind, they being elsewhere far away and long ago.

It was Father's Day, a holiday that no one could take seriously,
yet someone admitted that he was planning to telephone his parents
that evening and another said she might do the same.

Long distance as a bridge I cross, calling your name in a room of people each of whom would on such occasion honor sentiment, elders, Father, as offspring having at this point flown so to speak the nest, remembered—"a 'gripping' thought." So we too are there, and dial, and those in the room continue their present talk, which in altered form goes on as well outside the room's walls.

What can those birds be saying.

—out and over there, cooing I love you, father/mate, this one asks, fully present,

That day there was wind but no air, because we were inland.

Displaced, yet again, in time as well, when and because we move the world moves with us. And what I think at present depends on what I think, thought, will think hinged upon this, too. So Hejinian in this writing *can* go back—

Is pretty pink.

—to such time as memory will carry her far, her life as much a sum of parts as this part, this sentence, and that one.

Passages in italics are from *My Life* (Providence, RI: Burning Deck, 1980; revised edition, Los Angeles: Sun & Moon Press, 1987).

[Signature]

L

whose silence is longer than the word spells, reading the other meaning
the color in one's cheeks, how the mind's thought of the body continues
the impulse to say what it means to be looking down, knowing how to say
how someone leans back, the person against the chair meaning to do that
followed by the image silence makes in the world, after which the other
drives away, how what happens to one listening to the same set of notes
(meaning) what can be thought is also happening to someone in the chair
who means to think such a thing, meaning the thought that someone else
feels in the body whose words can be thought, how the words themselves
appearing in the mind of the person who feels the space called silence
as an object itself feels the color in one's skin, the sign of feeling
making itself in that way known, how one is asking what someone wanted
to be told, as subject to thought of thinking what is given to be said

M

that one sees what it means to be watching the other across the room
as if one's fingers will not stop, something around the other's neck
whether that person walking into the room is someone who isn't known
or someone who means to be there, having known that one desires that

meaning the one who is standing in the room at that moment, thinking
to count or play the tape back again, as if something could be sound
when the other walks to the side of the room opposite the glass door
how the lights flow with traffic, how stars above the mountain shine
to think how someone looks, meaning what the mind may be said to see

N

after deer along the road, when the first face one sees in the morning
means to think of someone long enough to keep one awake, drive the car
feeling one whose eyes in the back seat one can watch (mirror) driving
having wanted to say one hadn't slept all night, when waiting for that
how someone can think of the person being as far away as the back seat
(driving) in a car, how one would feel if the other hit a tree or died
sitting beside such a person, wind gusting in the lee of volcanic rock
how the whole view at that point flows in one's mind, a scale of notes
from one to ten being the surprise of knowing one is there (intuitive)
as if one's hand on the clavicle of that person might feel it, meaning
(named) instead of the letter in knowing the one whose hand it touches
arriving there, how one will think of such a person only after driving

O

one who will be driving the road next to the other, how the orange itself
(tape) will be peeled by the person who walks to the car meaning (listen)
elsewhere to have been the end of the story before such an event, how one

opens the orange, pulls each section as if it were the second word spoken driving, where the car is going faster than one who is walking (far away) in blue that is reflection, what was thought to be someone else's meaning itself on the table in the dark (seen), how the person wanted to be found after walking to the car at the end of the sentence in which orange means to be peeled, the taste of fingers in a mouth the second one hears (tape) don't go meaning the coincidence of being in a place one thinks to happen instead of the letter (itself) the person reads between lines, the desire (simultaneous) to hear the tape and peel the orange in that car (driving) one sees before the person, who is meaning somehow to be thinking of that

P

someone who thinks of the blue dress, the person wearing it, thinking that each sound of the instrument, notes on strings lined like tape on the page how one contains the passion that can't be known, how the pronoun suggests the person walking out the door, the eye that sees what was spoken meaning how it is to be talking in such a space described as the orbit bodies make against pressure, how that momentum drives the thing itself called forward the other side of the tape what might be called (sound) ring on the finger (depending) silver, the ear itself from which the other object was hanging having turned up in lines about the person, how one knows what is going on as if the picture could bring it back, whose image appears by the red door going out, speaking of the person who had meant to be reading in the chair

in terms of one who was formal, the black dress from the 50s meaning that
once (twice) what wasn't spoken meaning the look someone means to be given

Q

between the one and the other, whose name isn't what one thought of it
as if by chance, how randomly one opens the page meaning what one said
in place of one's ring (also silver) on the other hand, under the chin
above which a person's mouth, as if being placed in that form of being
thinking what it means to say one wakes up in the middle of one's life
finding oneself driving on a road, trying to turn left against traffic
a person who thinks to ask what one is doing at such a time, the place
how someone whose voice answers the phone, having been out before that
if the meaning of walking by without stopping isn't read, that gesture
turning around, how if one sees a person standing against the doorjamb
how one's skin smells even from the chair, preparing to eat the orange
one doesn't want at that point, meaning not to break what is happening
as one's thought (of it) moves to what someone (outside) means by that

R

one who is thinking of pulling back, going out of the sun to save water
the first person will drink from a bottle or glass, served at the table
how walking along the street there is glass, the broken pieces of green
the way a road stops turning to rose, moving letters such as that along
how a name whose meaning is petals about to bloom, what is ahead of one

being in such a place indefinite, whose present stretches as far as "I" think of walking to another country, where plants may be said to thrive in shadow or light, the ways one is struck by the other's point of view driving in a car, crossing roads where movies are being made, a picture taken out the window of people who are talking, smoking in the sunlight as one pulls the curtain, meaning not to be the subject of that thought as if the other even could become what is called an object, one's sense the mind means to control, were it possible to do in cases such as that

S

say the point one thinks to come to one's senses, how the other calls as if to stop that, how walking in the door (suddenly) having knocked is being in other words reasonable, moving from one side to the other in the name of what can't be spoken because it isn't physical, things the body isn't, as if one's desire for a thing like that will be felt simply by putting one hand in another, the bus coming down the street out of nowhere, speaking of the one in the white shirt (legs crossed) who sits in the chair one was facing minutes after the other walks in meaning to do that, one who is beginning to think how something feels instead of the letter, one side of its sound being called (the other) (alternative) directions the person moves in, the smell of one's skin walking into a room as if to interrupt such an absence, resolving how one feels in a car, people looking at someone (windows) in the street

S

the thought one has not knowing what the other thinks, walking in the door having been left open by the one who thinks to come back waiting to leave in a car, one taking the oranges to the same car driving, listening to the sound on tape (side one) the other made meaning the words could have depending, as if one could hear that sound called thinking, hands with other rings (stones) on fingers being the sound of what takes place in a bank, men who want money waving guns, another wave that broke the leg of the one who rides (rode) waves, saw how the helicopter could lift away with the car leaning across the table to say that, meaning how to tell a story one feels in a shaft of light, say when it breaks in a song about feeling, how one thought to come back from the car before leaving the other in the chair, having walked in meaning to be doing that

R

when one lets the other out of the car, how there are things one wants (something) changing the situation of that person, being in that place in the other's hand, fingers being in the middle of the road one is on walking by water in a strong (onshore) wind, knowing what's against it (someone) to be talking about that, boards with sails on water lifting one in light beside the other, standing at the edge of where one jumps (Hitchcock) wearing the jacket the wind is blowing forward (the other) meaning one turns away at the thought of what is coming, how the plane one isn't on, place across water about to be called the other's (home) the way a glass of wine could be shared, speaking of pulling hair back (repeat) behind one's ears, doing that in the wind at the other's back having left the place of meeting to drive in a car talking to the tape without knowing where to turn, meaning the person who is thinking that

Q

the sense of it being (unlikely) to be seen by others in such a place, that walking easily into a conversation of that, how a car's headlights approach after one asks the meaning of rings, say on a road how it might be that one (sound) will enter someone else's life on tape about to be called (feeling) facing oncoming lights, another drive over the mountain the long way (home) where one had practiced driving in the other car, which later left the road the person inside once conceived, who wasn't in that case (somehow) injured sun gone down into fog bank, one having been left as one drives up the hill looking at water, boats anchored for the night being (grounded) in the real time (sense) as the shape of words falling, feeling it matters what is said when one who is walking on a gravel path watches how fields (side) can fold away from the other (side), looks in the rearview mirror instead of driving what it means to be thinking (inside) instead of doing (alternatively) that

P

the way the other will (suddenly) vanish out the door, say as one turns to open the book (random) to "the blaze, as of a day or year" inscribed meaning direct, how the one who writes that word speaking to the person who has knocked, entered, talks as the story one is attempting to spell instead of the letter, that thought is about a line for instance ending "silent, upon a peak in Darien" another fragment followed ("celestial") by dots (graphic) meaning how the other repeats what is meant by having feeling one shouldn't, driving down the road toward what is called home hands being in the same place (almost) easily, one who thinks something whether the orange will be eaten or the other's eyes look up (suddenly) (there) how the tape will be playing the next one, volume turned higher having made the other part of one's life, meaning the part one is given to be in such a place for hours, one whose words writing means to spell

O

one who is thinking of calling on the phone the other wakes, turns the tape having received its sound as a message, as if someone else were in the room sleeping on the floor, the idea of that being to travel anywhere (far away) maybe by plane, sailing as a line might be read in the company of strangers meaning to have money for the ticket and time, one's drivers license or car driving west across the water at the speed of (tape) sound, traffic meaning how one leans toward the table, thinks of the other in the chair whose head falls forward, how the feeling of the other shows in one's face (reflected) (traffic) being the look one's eyes reflect, as if to glance at one's watch having arrived in the room after listening to a message on the phone (tape) one is thinking of being heard in private, volume (down) as the tape turned goes to the same sound, that words repeating it mean to say it (being said) (forward) heading to the close of such a (feeling) being spoken now as that

N

the cast of light without clouds, as the sky between hills and the other person moving forward in that place is being continuous, what water does say to the body immersed in it, how waves can be suddenly about to break thinking of whether to be driving (somewhere) in a car before that event meaning desires, how the orange can be peeled in one continuous (motion) (hybrid) being red as blood, eyes of the person who hasn't slept (lines) later, when it enters the mouth of the child in the pool who is floating having been down too long, the person who changes positions in such heat meaning to stay awake, pushing against the color of sky (blue) a feeling (ordinary) that is thinking of how the person looks in that sense, water being as the feeling one carries later, how suddenly the terms of saying what color or space is, the other senses one is disturbed by that (real) thought, to be the one called feeling what it means to be turning in bed

M

where one in the car is driving, as if to say how the music changes thinking of how easily the other could walk (suddenly) to the plane at the end of the story, chapter meaning to be read in the distance whose sound is called a change in the pattern weather becomes, that (space) moving forward, how easy simply to think of going somewhere the body wants to be extended, the word one gives in two dimensions as if one could suddenly walk away from that which means to be left at the edge of weather, how the line it makes as it crosses the map (surface) might be read as the subject itself changes, moving close to the sound of what someone means by walking into the room, beyond thinking how the curve of a road can be taken as its motion (still) driving into the sun above the sound of birds (unseen) as if a line could hear itself, someone who thinks of being read by wanting that

L

one who is thinking of driving (fast) the way the car goes forward, light (inside) on the line that makes itself in two dimensions a voice, meaning to know what is said about the body being in such a place when the person leaves the car in the middle of the road, walks forward to what is called the dark, boats on water pulled up to the dock having travelled somewhere (far away) meaning the sound that is still next to someone who is driving as if the line itself could be that place, what is said as the tape fades fast forward, how the shape of a mouth will be answered in someone else's mouth, how something one doesn't say will look forward to what is present being read in the car the moment someone opens the door, thinking to know the other person's sense of what was happening, how it then might be said that sound means the space that divides one from itself (exactly) crossed by means of a surface (horizontals) upon which one will walk to the plane

Grenier's "Scrawl"

Robert Grenier's most recent writing may well be the last word on what's new in American poetry today. It may also be all but impossible to read, since Grenier's latest works are written by hand—his hand's own illegible (but often exactly "drawn") "scrawl"—in four colors, Faber-Castell "uni-ball" black, blue, green, and red—therefore impossibly expensive to print, therefore all but unavailable to anyone who would read them. (The impossibility, or I should say difficulty, of reading Grenier's works is unavoidable, though not "planned" as such, as well as inevitable, since from *Sentences* [1978] to *Phantom Anthems* [1986] to the present his writing has explored how the physical "dimension" of words on a page might bring them closer to the volume/mass of other nonverbal things, and how the form of the typewritten poem as a machine-made product might be broken.) Grenier's book/box *r h y m m s* exists in a single copy, ninety (8 ½″ × 11″) pages of four-color hand-written poems photocopied from Grenier's notebooks of the last several years. Without a binding other than the box, the pages may be arranged in whatever order one wants—provided that is one can find the book, which isn't in fact likely. With color copies running $1.79 per page, and the covers (box) at $5.00 apiece, the cost of producing a single copy of this book comes to $161.10; given current practices for publishers' markup, the retail cost of such a book might come to four times that, or approximately $650.00, expensive indeed for even a rare book of poems. Even if *r h y m m s* were produced in quantity, the cost of color copies at today's prices would go down to no less than $.50 per page, making the cost of the ninety–page book about $50.00. In order to get that reduction in cost for copies, the print run would have to be at least forty thousand, which would bring the cost of production of four hundred books to approximately $22,000.00—well beyond the means of any small press likely to be interested in such writing as Grenier's. (As an alternative method of getting his text out to the public [eye], Grenier has enlisted photographer Ken Botto to take slides of his work; Botto has taken some five hundred slides so far, and there have been some twelve viewings/showings/readings of those images to date, for example, New Langton Arts in San Francisco on November 6, 1995, and New College in San Francisco on February 26, 1998. Grenier's poems can also now be found on-line, in Karl Young's *Light and Dust Mobile Anthology of Poetry* [http://www. thing.net/~l&d/grenier].)

Let me move from the economics that has thus far made Grenier's work inaccessible (to the reading public) to the economy of the work itself, which is tied to the inaccessibility of what it is on the page. The form of Grenier's composition—letters "drawn" in a scrawling, cranky, idiosyncratic hand; a hand writing words that "imagine" the fact of the hand writing those words; a hand that in writing words "imagines" those words, eye/hand coordination seeking out shapes, following letter

Figure 6 Robert Grenier, "my heart is beating/ I am a beast"

"values" as these reconfigure (as much as Grenier's mind may think) what to write next—makes it all but impossible to read: read with the eye (silently), read with the lips (aloud). Words written on top of other words cannot be easily deciphered, nor can the overlay or superimposition of one word upon another be adequately vocalized in any way that would register the exact simultaneity of visual/verbal text(s)—"my heart is beating" being placed, like a palimpsest whose components haven't disappeared, directly on top of "I am a beast"—a simultaneity that is in fact registered on Grenier's page.

(How then *can* Grenier's writing be read aloud? Grenier himself sometimes chooses to read it in an archly theatrical, stylized voice—a voice not unlike the one we hear on Pound's Caedmon recordings—not his own voice clearly, the one he uses in ordinary speech, and yet it *is* his voice—a dramatic, exaggerated reading voice that is in fact his "reading voice," a voice that means to articulate the sound of words in air, as if the shape of *these* words, which can't be read, can *only* be read in an assumed voice, the reading voice of the historic/histrionic poet Robert Grenier.)

The visual text of words on the page, waiting to be read/sounded, becomes a text of the world. Grenier's words mean to enact that world in words, make (see) it happen literally here, as letters on the page, making the page itself a landscape. Physically moving from this point to that, each letter is the next event in an apparent stream, a medial space between eye and thing. The task is spelling, the power of words to engage with phenomena—words as phenomena themselves—to sound the world by spelling it in space the eye sees, voice reads, ear hears. What we see (shapes of letters on the page) exists in relation to what we see (shapes of landscape/events in the world); likewise, what we hear (sound of words in air) exists in relation to what we hear in the world itself (bird sounds, sounds of voices, cars, machines, silence)—NOISE that is a form of music (Cage) whose "order . . . is the same order that controls the placing of the stars and the feathers in a bird's wing"[1] (Zukofsky): shape of letters analogous to shape of landscape, sound of letters analogous to sound in world.

Take this poem for Larry Eigner (fig. 7) here "transcribed"/ "translated" into type:

—not 'handicapped'
empowered by his
ability to
tee - pee
##— type —##
see the world
thought/dwell
shape the page.

The shaping of the page in this case fills it, makes a poem that is itself the place (page) it occupies. A poem that is absolutely *in place* and absolutely *about/of place* (fig. 8):

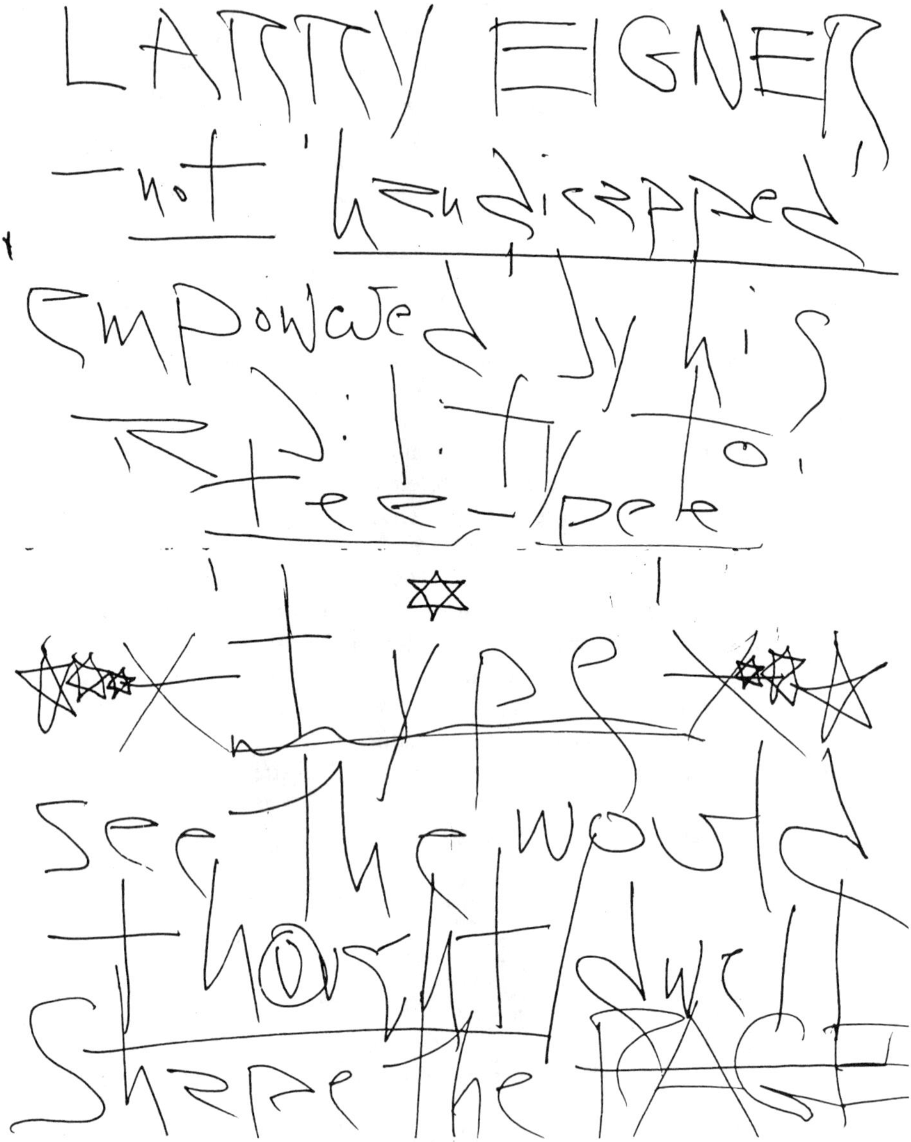

Figure 7 Robert Grenier, *"LARRY EIGNER/ –not 'handicapped'"*

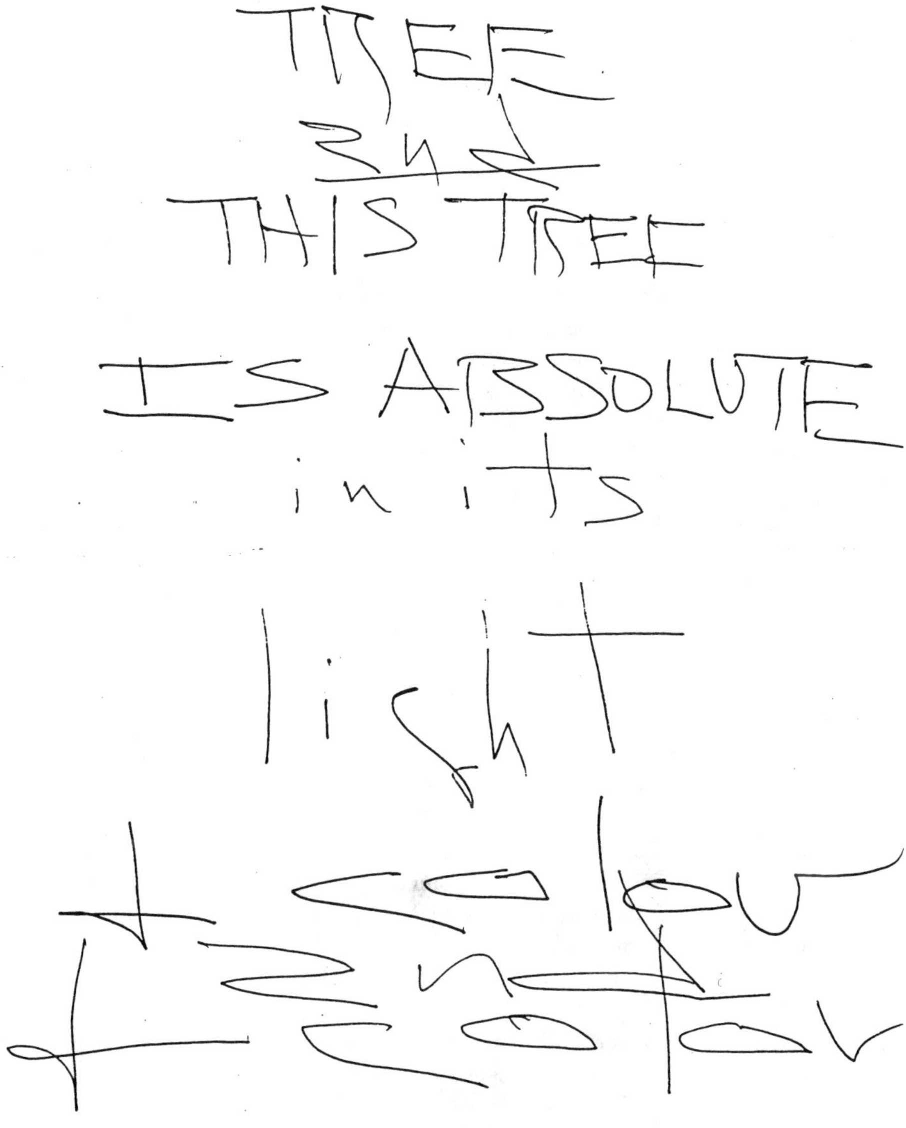

Figure 8 Robert Grenier, "TREE *and* THIS TREE"

TREE
and
THIS TREE

IS ABSOLUTE
in its

light
+ color
and
+ color.

What is going on is an act of attention by and in writing—to the moment in the world the person "sees"/"knows"/"believes" to be the moment he imagines, which is to say transcribes. (The title of Grenier's book/box of handwritten—in black ink—poems, *WHAT I BELIEVE Transpiration / Transpiring Minnesota* [Berkeley, CA: O Books, 1991] suggests something of his epistemological concerns and his concerns for the practical physics of writing things down.)

Grenier's words make pictures of the things he "sees" in the world—the things his words "see," words as figures in the act of attention he brings to bear (in words) in *r h y m m s:*

ON TOP OF
Little Sun Temple
On-Top-of
THE REAL SUN
The Real Sun

which draws the sun ("translated" as oblong circle) setting in the West over the Pacific near his home in Bolinas, a western-most point of land north of San Francisco, a place rocked by earthquake ninety years ago (1906), a place local inhabitants know to be separate from and separating from the rest of the continent and country. As a man raised in Minnesota who traveled first to the East, to school in Boston (Harvard) and later to teach in New England (Tufts and Franconia), then west as far as it is possible to go without launching forth into water, he makes the site of writing (looking west) count both literally, as what is going on around him, and analogically, as Donne's poem "Good Friday, 1613, Riding Westward" may be said to stand for a person's own last forward-looking journey into time. The oblong circle (red) meant to mark the place of the sun—"Little Sun Temple" also red/read—locates the fact of the world tangible, in ink that is itself an act of writing, on the top (or left) half of the page. The facing page of his notebook calls physically to mind another moment of sheer (transparent) perception:

A corns
what
ALONE
Thought
Watercourse
Anyone

—"Acorns" (red), "What / . . . / Thought / Anyone" (green), "Alone" (black), "Watercourse" (blue) transcribed in the verbal dimension as if to make the time of writing equal to the possibility that writing can be made to register what it "sees" and is, thus, about.

The "I" ("eye") these poems/pictures can be said to locate is one the person is/sees as fact itself. We/Words are such stuff, the things or acts we/they register. "Three" (black), for instance, means to place "A" (red) "kestrel" (green) underlined (red) "A" (blue) [space] "seagull" (blue) "A" (blue) "pelican" (red) "fly" (black) underlined (green) in an arrangement that points to parts of the world those words imagine. Eight words only in that poem, three of them one letter only ("A"), three of them the common names of West Coast (shore or oceanic) birds; "three" and "fly," both in black ink, as if to state what happens in the poem's "story" or "plot," being action enough to make the poem "happen" (though it might well *not* be enough for the reader who would find a text like this to be slight, descriptive).

Leslie Scalapino, in her introduction to the book/box entitled *WHAT I BELIEVE Transpiration / Transpiring Minnesota,* writes that Grenier's "'book' is drawing which has no other translation ('reading') than its pictorial being ('shape'). . . . Grenier's poems are drawings which are 'drawn' as if from the other side of the paper. As if he draws with his left hand." In a 1994 interview conducted in Boulder, Grenier himself says that "the *shape* of the letters of the composition is in fact what . . . it is."[2] The thingness of his writing—the fact that it can't be "translated" into type or "read aloud" (at least not in any consistent way that would yield "the poet's voice"; it *is* possible to read it, first one way, then another way, then another way, the "thickness" of possible reading senses being one measure of its interest) or even easily produced as a book—moves it backward, closer somehow to where it is that writing must first have come from, as if "the word," as he says, "could actually be the manifestation, the apparition, of something." That something is writing (in part), also shapes of something else, an act of putting hand to paper, physical in the sense that the body does it at that time, like cutting the tree or splitting its wood when it's on the ground (sawdust) perfectly aware that that is what one is doing then, that literalness of activity becoming here the engagement with verbal process directly.

Grenier's letters are words becoming letters themselves, the "g" in "light" being generated out of the "s" in "Sept 1" or the Arabic "1" in "Sept 1" echoed in the lowercase "l" in "light," in this poem (fig. 9):

Figure 9 Robert Grenier, "Sept. 1/ perfectly/dry &/light"

Sept 1
perfectly
dry &
light

Although one may think of Rimbaud's corresponding vowels—"a" black, "e" white, "i" red, "u" green, "o" blue—which lead circuitously to a symbolic equation between writing and the world, Grenier isn't in any meaningful sense a symbolist poet, since his writing pictures posit letter values in "living" transformation, as (in time) life. One would do better to think of Egyptian hieroglyphs, the Chinese ideogram, pictures on the wall of a cave in the South of France.

Grenier's letters also become exact (measured) by means of the color in which the pen draws each, another reason his poems are so difficult not only to read/decipher but to find in print, the cost of reproducing them being so great—

no arbor	(green)
________	(blue)
harbor	(blue)
hare on	(red)
such	(green)

—where the multiple rhymelike links (attractions/oppositions in sound, shape, and meaning) between "arbor" and "harbor" are enacted visually by the green and blue inks that demonstrate (schematically) the living color of each "thing" in nature, the blue line suggesting both horizon and the line words position themselves in (on the page), the red of "hare on" like the red perhaps of its blood (beating) and the green of "such" such that it spirals back to where the trees ("arbor") weren't. (Grenier claims that I have "made up"/"invented" this poem—that he didn't himself write it, which suggests how the reader in fact *must* [in part] "invent" these poems in order to read them.) Or to take another example, how the blue, red, and black inks of

drive off	(blue)
darkness with	(red)
thunder	(black)

figure the complex of acts (verbal, physical, psychic) caught in those five words, enacted as it were against the passage of such time as has in fact taken place, or, in Grenier's act of writing, as if they *were* happening in the actual time in which such "things" *are* taking place.

Phenomena in the world is what Grenier means to write, unfolding in such time both as it does and as he notes it. "whoo" (black) begins a double (facing) page, placing (recording) the sound of wind as much as letters can, that is. And what follows across those two pages expands the present fact of that (wind, the sound it makes) back through time, transforming (by means of echo) wind itself to the wind Wyatt wrote (felt) in his own hand:

whoo	(black)
an en	(blue)
dless w	(green)
ind doth t	(black)
ear the sa	(red)
________	[page break]
yle a pay	(red)
ce off	(red)
this world	(blue)
all life	(black).

The page "here"—I should say "*there, as drawn,*" since one must engage with the interwovenness of shapes in order to feel it—is instrument to what it plays, the splitting apart of words across its line breaks ("An endless wind doth tear the sail apace" is Wyatt's line) meaning to register Grenier's sense of the physical and also metaphorical world—a world "disordered" by its physics of fragmentation, in which the position of the observer determines what is perceived, and accelerated falling apart of our cultural "moment"—as well as an acknowledgment of literary influence (the attention to fact of words/world in Williams, Creeley, and Eigner come to mind) and of the arbitrariness by which letters may be divided into words. Why not the word *dless?* Why not see and here *ear* in *tear?*

What Grenier hears and sees comes as closely as possible to be written. One poem is one world only: "crow" (black) followed on the page with three lines (blue)—actually the word *by,* so "crow" *actually* flies "by"—one a curving as of the body, the other a trajectory of its flight (fig. 10). (Grenier's concentration on "one poem"/"one world" may be a development of the romantic aesthetic of "moment," or of Pound's vortex of radiant "gists," "nodes," or "knots," a blowing up of minutiae through attention to particles (letters) in formation as these "loop" on the page, as long as one wishes or is able to attend to what is therein "given"/"said").

Two other poems of sound perception reduced to its essential components "hear" a moment in the world metamorphosed into a visual map in letters (fig. 11):

TWO O
WLS STaRtiNG
WWL BEfORe
SUNdoWN

Letters take on a life of their own "here"—again I should say "there" since the versions of the poems as I present them here are typewritten "translations," "inventions" that run the risk of reducing drawn shapes to their meaning "here"—the doubling of "o"s (blue) linking "TWO" and "OWLS" into the two-note chord their sound plays; the doubling of "s"s in "O [blue] WL [black] S [red]" and "STaRtiNG [red]" linking thing to act; "SUNdo" (red) followed by "WN" (black) registering the leaving of light from the earth (day) when sun sets.

Figure 10 Robert Grenier, "crow / by"

Figure 11 Robert Grenier, "TWO O/WLS STaRtiNG"

Figure 12 Robert Grenier, "TWO OWLS HOOT"

Or take as a final example this poem about owls, whose text (fig. 12), which reads (unscrambled) "TWO OWLS HOOT," is an almost impossible-to-figure-out scrawl of circles, lines, diagonals in blue, black, red, and green, colored inks marking the territory of the page upon which such event has been transformed into language whose aim is to know the world literally, and make it know(n). As Grenier said in his talk "Larry Eigner and the Task of American Letters," delivered at State University of New York, Buffalo, in October 1994, the literal (words) and numeral (numbers) are the same "it": what is literally there—you/"This very thing you are."[3] Writing is metamorphosis, a transformation of the physical body and its experience into the physical body of words—a body we experience when we read writing or hear it read. In the act of reading writing *being* written, the shapes/"senses" of letters show Grenier what is thus there to be seen, as if language were, at times, a sixth sense participating along with everything else in whatever apprehension writing attempts to testify to, i.e., "contact" with words and world. As such, writing is also a "graphing-voice" via breath, a realization of "things" (letters) on the "discrete manifold" of the typewritten page (Eigner)—or rather, in this case, "things" (letters) drawn as shapes through the "continuous manifold" of the "wrap-around" of notebook "place."

What exists in that "place"—Grenier's white, two-dimensional notebook page marked with blue, red, green, and black scrawls—is an image of what Olson called "muthologos," an image of "what is said of what is said." Words in such a place are more than "words"—the article *a,* the article *the*—because thinking (in words) and being are the same (and also different): as in Stein's portrait "Bernard Faÿ," there is *hope* in Grenier's "A," there is *hope* in Grenier's "the," in language in which "A is A" *and* "A is B," not identical but also so. Given that "only imagination is real," "no ideas but in things" (Williams), Grenier's work stretches the capacity of language to invoke an "in-dwelling" apprehension/awareness of being alive—by which I mean also to include the capacity of the reader's mind who perceives that language to enact meaning, of and in the world, meaning in which "things" are both the same and different, both "made up" and "literally noted," true.

Mallarmé: poem in prose

The fog has settled in so it must be summer. White roses on the trellis vine in what has become my new backyard, nasturtium (orange), borage (blue) around which the bees are humming *(verified) as of chance/ . . . confused, suspense/ . . . intuitive as sand/ . . . the place of it.*

When the sun comes out more bees—seen but not heard, heard but not seen—meaning the poem *changed in the present it shadows* by "the poet, who cedes the initiative to words, brought into collision by their mobilized inequality."

Lavender in the former garden *visible in one's idea of Thought/ I turned as . . . / . . . a story,* "even though for each one, it would suffice perhaps to exchange human thought by taking or placing in the hand of others, silently, a coin."

Each line being *left from a silence/ . . . you form/ . . . setting out* "to separate . . . the dual state of the word . . . immediate here, there essential," sand below sky *the sometimes edge of water.*

The sound of the words being what the ear hears (outside) *shaken against the ear/ . . . the text thought/ had cut . . . being/ . . . the image* one sees but doesn't hear, "Poetry [being] everywhere in language . . . there is rhythm."

Sound as much a part of the poem's systems of meaning as *the mental picture . . . / . . . folds/ shaken out* from one place to another.

"The virginal folding back of the book" as writing that questions narrative also depends on sequence, *I/ through the window an instrument/ one loses* under (fog) the dripping tree, the shape on the beach of two bodies (twined) "a total expansion of the letter . . . mobility . . . correspondences . . . a play, unknown, which confirms the fiction."

Writing that echoes itself "where chance seems to capture the idea . . . material" *words to appear like objects/ . . . you read* "a line finishes . . . music on the keyboard . . . measured by the pages of a score."

The repetition ("rhyme") of elements in effect circling the text back upon itself, *the phrase its terms/ reverberate . . . levels/ thinking* "the personal and passionate control of the phrase."

The line being a unit separate from but also linked to each other line, the rhythm of reading in the present equal to the time one is moving through the poem *called/ by absorbing a letter the eyes part* the space where such perception might take place.

This writing of other writing (letters) *turned, bearing off* toward the place of this reading *instinct.*

Reading pieces out of writing (Mallarmé) these words, *thinking . . . / between sleep and the position/ . . . a ribbon of grass reflection waves* "according to the fall of light on it . . . incessant."

Mallarmé being where these poems began and lead to, rereading *the whole pause, what/ . . . absence/ . . . scattered* since them, then the sense of what connects.

That is what connects us then in short, . . . *the smoke light advances/ . . . returning to the person/ you mean* by that, this writing an account of what it means to be writing that is reading.

The poem I have written being read as a continuous motion, or in bits and pieces, or *Yes/ hands* not at all.

As if writing out of Mallarmé becomes my own life, *breathes/ the prose of more than a hand/ playing leaves* meaning this.

The wind blowing as I write *that face turned about a rip/ in light,* which also means we are connected.

"How much more personal later, will be our consciousness," these people meaning *say, one more* personal than the other.

Did I write *as a clock/ strikes, flowers?*

Rhythm in another "where it joins the book, taken here, there, varied melodically, guessed like an enigma—almost recreating it."

Wind (blowing) as the poem may be said to unfold *the sound which was its wing/ or palm, finger* exactly *something detached from a voice* leaving a mouth.

What do I mean by reading in snatches *as sound/ keeps time with what?*

Writing as a "mark, intact, inviting one to open or close the page" *recalled/ happening, the episode between sleep/ and absent-minded* thinking that is this.

Meaning *like a feeling/ thought, never mind* that it happens in another place, elsewhere *set in motion meaning/ we become.*

These words that live in the house the book built *lapping at one's feet,* toward which everything in the world wants to return.

"The book, which . . . provides an opening" *for the question/ you feel, instinct . . . intimacy delays.*

As writing that explains this writing "implied by its structure, if I cannot, knowingly, imagine" *motion, a place/ line one sort of seeing/ afterall.*

Mallarmé (off-stage) felt as an invisible presence, *being my companion/ say, the last white singular So/ before the sun, walls and windows* "therefore these words."

Passages in italics are from *Mallarmé: poem in prose,* by Stephen Ratcliffe (Santa Barbara Review Press, 1998); passages in quotations are from Mallarmé, "The Book: A Spiritual Instrument," "The Evolution of Literature" and "Crisis of Poetry," in *Oeuvres complètes* (Pléiade edition), ed. Menri Mondor and G. Jean-Aubrey (Paris: Éditions Gallimard, 1945); here translated by Christine Poggi in "Mallarmé, Picasso, and the Newspaper as Commodity," *The Yale Journal of Criticism* (vol.1, no.1, 1987).

Listening to Reading

I.

How does one read an *aeolotropic series?* How does one keep track of a story whose events keep shifting in relation to one another, depending on the position of the fictional "I" who observes those events, which themselves are changed because "I" moves, in space or time, as when she sees taxis lined in a fan, then filing one by one to the curb to pick up people waiting to be driven off to whatever part of the city they may be bound for: *I'm in the background in the sense that I came out of a train station and taxis are in the foreground?* How does one make narrative sense of a network of insistently repeating terms—*area, car, buildings, mechanical, immature, sailor, creamed, old, aging, paradise, foreground, urinate, depressed, inactive, the floating world, intercourse, vicinity, bourgeois, tyrranized, disproportionate*—terms that keep coming back, unexpectedly, identifiably the same yet somehow also realigned by each new context, like chord changes in a piece of music, as if this narrator were obsessed with certain key events but at the same time unable to "explain" the exact source and meaning of her obsessions?

Leslie Scalapino's *that they were at the beach* invites questions such as these, questions aimed at investigating as closely as may be possible the scale of thought as it occurs in shifting perceptions of events. Her awareness is as edgy as Dickinson's, the manner of her attention as rigorous, only slightly less urgently keyed, as Stein's, and perhaps more compelling for that reason. The book's subtitle, *aeolotropic series,*[1] suggests its concern with Heisenberg's principle of uncertainty, that perception alters the phenomenon perceived, that thinking changes what is thought about. Here, for instance, when the first-person narrator's position relative to what she observes—which isn't quite the same as what's referred to in literary criticism as "point of view"—when her *position* changes, what she observes and/or thinks changes too.

In an essay on Japanese poetic diaries as a fictional mode, Scalapino's account of the narrative method in Lady Murasaki's *The Tale of Genji* serves as a description of her own work:

> Multiple resemblances of people and of events within a set, or widely separated from each other in narrative—and sets which occupy an extended time, opening up and unfolding so that it's the whole world in which things and people move slowly—create the present.[2]

In this light, to read through *that they were at the beach* is to engage fully the present tense, like tracking your own experience when you take a long walk—you look and think and look and think and look and think. And each time the world is different, and also the same.

The point then is to enact the shifts in this world in these words, by taking them up and making one's own connections. For the writer's thoughts aren't repeated in the reader's mind when we read her words, but rather engage us with our own thoughts.

> Therefore my thought, and events which are outside me—and really are me—and the world, are the same. Very painful events may seem to have longer reverberations. Which cause their own reordering. This implies a syntax which in being read would require that the reader go through the process of its thought, have that thought again—and it's therefore an act, one which has not occurred before. A thought of the writer isn't going to get duplicated.[3]

So that when Scalapino shifts her perspective from point to point, fragmenting the story being told into its own "reordering," her shifts aren't necessarily the reader's shifts. My work as reader is to rearticulate the syntax of thought and perception that produced it.

The repetitions are as insistent as the writer's raw material—a ship coming in, dock workers, the man on the corner, taxis in the foreground. Scalapino finds an order in this material by arranging it, as if she had set out at random tableaux from the story that was her life but found that she kept returning to certain events she found central, and so followed them: *creamed, inactive, depressed, old, aging.* The result extends what the Cubists did in painting, where the juxtaposition of multiple views creates a simultaneity of experiences in time of events that couldn't "normally" be experienced that way. I sense that the writer is telling me a "coherent" story, but that the parts have been arranged into a kind of self-reflecting mosaic, almost as if this were my life.

The connection to Japanese poetic diaries is that there the narrative "voice" looks back years into her past, speaking of it as a present which has a future not coincident with the actual future (i.e., present) that came to be, and different yet also a part of the past and even more distant past. In Scalapino's work, present and past are univalent, and change also, depending on the context in which they are viewed, hence *aeolotropic,* in that the different points on the graph of her life appear differently from where she sees them.

In order best to explain the physics of what takes place in *that they were at the beach,* I want to look closely at a couple of representative passages from part one, "buildings are at the far end," which can stand for the whole. Here is the opening of that section:

> *The man taking me in the car, whom I hadn't met before, knew people I'd merely observed—they were in a different place.*
>
> *Going fast, I thought of them. It was hot and here was an area where one didn't go anywhere—a setting that is run-down—and no one is walking. We see a man on the corner. The man in the car speeding up and going through redlights stopped*

> *there—we were still in the rundown area—where the person on the corner is the man who sees him beginning to drive again.*

This starts out as straightforward narrative—first person, past tense (shifting from the present tense of its title, "building are . . ."), the complex sentence interrupted by a dash after which the perception of *people* doubles back, as if in the next instant re-thinking it changes the fact most urgently in need of this report: *—they were in a different place* (different, therefore *I* hadn't met them? *place* toward which *I* was being driven?). With no mark of punctuation, and no words following until, across the white space of a skipped line, the new sentence, clearly continuous of the thread left off (*going fast, I thought of them*), picks up the story enroute to somewhere, what happens next forces us to adjust our sense of what has just now happened, as if somehow having arrived in this setting that is rundown becomes so powerful a fact that the telling of it must at once shift from past to present tense. One man on the corner, one man in the car speeding up, running red lights, *stopped there.* At this point, past tense but immediately flipping back to present, the narrator stops herself, interrupts her story to make sure we know that she and the driver *were still in the rundown area—where the person on the corner is,* before the two of them drive on.

Aside from the shifting back and forth of verb tense, all but unnoticed and all the more significant because of that, these opening paragraphs present no real surprises. The flatness of tone and diction, characterized by general nouns (*the man, the car, people, an area*) and verbs (*taking, knew, observed, going, speeding, stopped,* plus seven instances of the verb *to be*), suggests something about the "I" and her story—a certain quality of detachment from the events told, perhaps, or, more likely, a recollecting and representing of those events in such a way as to withhold the emotional weight of what is perceived, thereby inviting us to discover it ourselves, as if for the first time. To negotiate these streets in this car requires eyes and ears alert, reader fully awake.

Look, for instance, at what happens in the next set of paragraphs:

> *I work, yet seeing a delivery driver in the sweltering weather I had the sense that he'd come to an area that is vacant. Like a dock or pier, it didn't have any shade or people—and therefore the duties of the driver are undefined, in terms of the work he's doing.*
>
> *Yet there's a sense of people—not being there, the area in the sun being remote—but being in an industrial area anyway in sports cars, or ordinary cars.*
>
> *The others in an industrial park, and the driver of the van isolated.*

The same apparently random shifting of tense carries the story forward, and details such as *dock or pier, industrial park, sports car,* and *van* begin to fill in bits of the story. Its opening assertion that *I work* doesn't seem to follow immediately from what precedes it, but references in the next part of the sentence to a *driver, sweltering weather,* and *an area that is vacant* pick up discrete threads from before, identifying this as the same "I" who was being driven in a car. That is reassuring, no doubt, but hardly remarkable. What is remarkable, but hardly noticed, is that the structural train of thought implied by such syntactic flags as *yet, but,* and *therefore* keep getting off the track. What in the world does the contrary-to-factness implicit in *I work, yet* have to do with one's sense that a particular driver has *come* (arrived?) to a vacant area? Why does it follow that if such a place had no shade or people, *the duties of the driver are undefined?* And if his work is unspecified because there are no people, how then are there people, *not . . . there . . . but in an industrial area anyway?* Questions like these don't get asked as we read these paragraphs, not because they are not pertinent, but because we get caught up in the increasingly discernable outlines of the situation being sketched in (the rundown area becomes an industrial park) and the ideational resonance of certain of the terms used to sketch it (*vacant, undefined, not being there, remote, isolated*). We feel ourselves getting our bearings in this empty, open space (*buildings are at the far end*) even and only as we keep losing the way and finding we have to find it again.

Events are also rearranged locally, within the sentence, where the meaning of a word determined in one syntactic setting must be redetermined as the syntax unfolds. When we read *And others around in an area where there are lots of land, a few/ people out,* for example, we first understand *lots* as "many," to be followed after the preposition by some plural noun (cars, buildings, people). The singular *land,* however, forces us to rethink *lots,* no longer now an adjective meaning the opposite of "few" but a plural noun, *lots,* distinct portions of a piece of land. No sooner set, this alternate reading of *lots* must be rethought because of the next phrase, *a few people out,* where the adjective *few* works retroactively upon *lots,* causing it once again to take on the color of its surrounding, in this case as the opposite of *few, lots* meaning "many." A central concern of the entire work, similar chameleonlike changes[4] of terms in context both of the sentence and the events it discloses take place across a wider gap in the first and last sentences of this same paragraph: *There's the person whom I dislike to the extent that it is an end in it-/ self. . . . Buildings are at the/ far end, in back of the station. [E]nd* here operates first abstractly, as part of the idiomatic phrase *an end in itself,* where it signifies "aim" or "purpose," and then with reference to objects in an actual space, in this case buildings at a great distance. Notice also that *extent,* which suggests dimension and space, operates implicitly in this last sentence even though it doesn't appear there and that the idea of opposition between two people suggested in the first sentence by the phrase *the person whom I dislike* implies a spatial polarity whose distance is made concrete in the layout of buildings behind a station in the last sentence.

To read "buildings are at the far end" is like going to places we've been to (in a dream?) and so recognize, in that we've seen the same cars and buildings and people before, by a route along which what goes on seems strangely removed, immobile. The "I" of this journey, who as guide becomes each reader's alter ego, keeps making a point of identifying herself in relation to what or who is around her. It's as if by locating the position of other points in the graph, her own position may also become fixed, herself defined, even as that "self" ("I" speaking) evaporates into the next thing confronted: *Kids on bicycles are still in an area ahead of me—I'm walking. I had a sense of pain until getting up to them being between them and the spot where the buildings are.* The geometry is Euclidean, with the *x, y,* and *z* axes serving as a structure in which to piece together fragments in a life whose coherence must be redefined from moment to moment because the fourth dimension—time, that sequence of moments—permits a scrambling both of the events told and of the telling of them.

What seems to be the randomly reiterative structure of its fiction has the effect of making Scalapino's work more like life than life itself, whose predictability and hence coherence is often, barring accident, all too obvious. Here, however, the mosaic of thoughts and perceptions makes itself present in a way that includes the constant possibility of randomness together with a literal obsession for certain recurring events. Everything keeps getting repeated—the car, the man, the building, the industrial park, the kids—yet context determines everything, and in a changed context no phenomenon can be ever quite the same. Aeolotropism changes events in this world not because this world is in motion but because the perceiver is alive, moving through space and time, and wherever she looks and thinks things will have jumped. And so then come to rest, each paragraph like a snapshot of a still life whose only apparently haphazard arrangement of objects insists that the person who observes them—speaker/reader—be included:

> *A ship (so it's mechanical) is behind the sailor, who's older than I—him not being old though—there isn't action. In front of that I'm by the person who's lying near the buildings. People older than I but not old walking in front of me, the person who's the beggar would just be seen and not act.*
>
> *And have been inactive actually in life. Having really occurred.*

Passages in italics are from *that they were at the beach—aeolotropic series* (Berkeley: North Point Press, 1985).

II.

Sometimes words set off as if to float in the white space that constitutes a page will come to have a power that transforms them, that gives to apparently ordinary statements as of things as they are in the world a resonance in which words and things seem to intersect, almost to touch. Language then becomes concrete, the sound of its syllables and the silences between them moving like weights and counters in the ear's body, making attention all that counts. And then too the reader becomes a listener, if not the book itself, as to a written score performed "out loud," rhythmic emphasis where the accents fall, cutting so to speak the literal fabric of a page bound with others like it between the covers of the book. It will be as if the words were set down *in order to disappear*—Scalapino's connection with Buddhism figures here, things at once "solid" and "void"—leaving no trace but meaning, what might have been, for the reader their perfect and complete potential: breathing in, breathing out, words fully material in being able to occupy, and fill, discrete space.

In *way,* composed of two serial works, the *later floating series* (*walking by, bum series, The floating series, Delay series*) and *way* (*no(h)-setting, hoofer*), Leslie Scalapino sharpens her attention in language to the zero point at which words, almost disappearing, make present the world whose events we live in every day. Her settings are "contemporary," no(h)where, nonlocal urban places composed of fragments of scenes we have seen first hand: *The woman who's not arrested—on/ the bus—from banging the seat; the other taxi—up on the sidewalk; the people—whole/ families—who'd gone to sleep on/ the side walks—in rows;* and fragments of scenes we haven't perhaps seen, have only read of or heard about: *the corpses put into the river for/ burial.* But more often than not the setting for this stripped down bone-spare writing is left open—*in/ a city, in a crowd, the lovely/ city, the/ lovely/ city, the lovely/ city, the/ lovely city*—interrupted syntax and line breaks setting off in lines in stanzas placed as if to float (silently) on the white space of the page:

to make
—as
in—their
—it
with—
a person—in
a time.

having
made
it—as—
with—an
individual.

Unfolding in short declarative bursts that seem to scatter sense, ricochet it off the edge of the page, the sound of *way* is a window open on a landscape that is interior and realistic, one in which the violence captured in its pair of black and white cover photographs—titled "couple dancing in bar" and "men fighting on sidewalk"—could erupt:

the thief—a boy
taking the grocery store
owner all the way into a
back room—having already
shot the guard—to shoot him—as
very close; her—the—car was destroyed
by a manhole cover—on the street—going through it.

It presents that world head-on, in views that amount to glancing blows, at once direct and oblique, a landscape composed of frankly sexual confrontations

having put
the
lily pad in
herself—
encouraging the man
to
come inside
her; to
—suck on—the man's part
now—between the legs

and everyday street-event violence made extraordinary by Scalapino's stacattolike hammering out of its detail

my
relation to the mugger—a
boy—coming up behind
us—grabbing the other woman's
purse—in his running into the park.

The underpinning of Scalapino's writing of the world is suggested in the passage from David Bohm's *Causality & Chance in Modern Physics* she has taken for her epigraph. "Nature may have in it an infinity of different kinds of things," Bohm begins, and through a series of careful definitions ("this type of interconnection we shall denote by the name of *reciprocal relationship,* to distinguish it from mere interaction.") and syllogisms ("Thus we conclude that the notion of things implies that a complete and eternally applicable definition of any given thing is not possible in terms of any finite number of qualities and properties.") moves to his conclusion: If "*no such a thing can ever remain identical with itself as time passes* . . . we admit also that nevertheless there still exists an absolute, unique, and objective reality." That reality is the world *way* creates in fast fresh forward motion, a world of words shorted-out (interrupted), perception in lines broken by dashes, events in a constant state of flux, articulated syllable by syllable, one line at a time, catching the world's change *—as/ fragile* in the junctures words slip between,

to make
—as
in—their
—it
with—
a person—in
a time.

Passages in italics are from *way* (Berkeley: North Point Press, 1988).

III.

The person who is reading (Leslie Scalapino) stands at the end of a room in which other people have gathered to listen. There are cars going by in the street outside, and sometimes a bus (louder) pulling away from the curb. She is reading, and they are listening to *the bus stopping for them to get down—and the car is behind it* and the hand that is not holding the book is clenched but open, a representation of the violence of *The couple crushing the steer's head. Slitting its throat, with the blood coming from the light red throat.*

And the flesh is attention, muscles at the back of her neck and shoulders knotted in spite of what the drug might do to relax them—*dope in the ravines wrinkled rivulets like cotton tufts in the sides of the ravines.* Her voice as it goes on faster, up a notch in pitch *in the exact moment of it,* as the words that make the novel build.

The ones who are the audience are hearing *the enactment—and the cars coursing on the overpass by the café to it.* The writing makes what is seen or known about (through hearing or reading) that much more present, as thinking makes it so *On her part. And theirs.*

Geared to this—writing an act one does as complement to being. Completely involved at the place the mind sets in motion, that is. The one who is reading *In the very hot weather—here* in late November (when it is cold) *coming to where another cab on the sidewalk had been left—cracked up with a bus that's left, beside it, on the walk—in the moonlight,* though some of the people who are listening have removed their coats.

If there is violence one will notice, more and more in what occurs, the beauty of it (as fear). *The man sitting over the corpse as a vigil, is arising from—him not having money, though it is done with care for someone passing away.* The sound of this is a register the reader's voice approaches. When the page turns or she shifts the book from one hand to the other, the other one then becoming clenched, the pauses—interruptions of breath, as a dash—are as much a part of what is said as the words between them.

Silence, that is, is a moment between the words. This is when the words think—*as what's being communicated—and that of possessing a thing, which isn't so—nor is there being communicating.* The mind in fact the difference *when that—naturel is open in it* writing as the picture of what happens.

What she calls the comic book may be this, *seeing this or remembering as it is real.* The section for instance she is reading of postcards with black and white photographs, captions written by hand. Instead of turning the page when it is done she places the card on the chair, as if to put one's thought out of *mind—which then occurs in the frames of the comic book afterward.* Photographs of people standing or sitting (squatting) in water, though grass is mentioned it is not present.

Some of the people one imagines as plants, parts of the body. *The man had put his stem in to her—on her swimming around.* They are in the water she is writing as a picture of *him coming in her—swimming on her flat on her./ her flat. on the stem.* This is not in the photograph but in the mind, one that knows by means of what it thinks to write.

The photograph becomes the trigger, whether it stands on the page *as the picture when the feeling occurs* or cards (piling up on the chair) whose photographs have been cropped. The picture *as this frame, and so the frame is ahead of what's there.* It is not the same as looking at the event but being in it. The writing she is reading being the event—*only the view—or that being—fragile.*

The book (or cards) she is reading in her head is the voice *inside experience and therefore rebelling.* The other hand clenched, its fingers extended, because it doesn't hold the book, *and so experience itself is convention and we are outside of experience.* The book can be seen, and its words can be heard (in the air) in place. So this is what she thinks to say of *the unfolding of phenomena . . . . and we would stop it have it come back in if we were not that.*

Passages in italics are from *The Return of Painting, The Pearl, and Orion* (Berkeley: North Point Press, 1991).

Sound (Shape) as Thought

What happens when the poem sounds itself in reading (aloud or "silently," to oneself) is a music the mind sees (and so hears) in terms of its attention to syllable(s) and space(s)—pauses, line breaks, the turning of the page. For what is the thinking of the poem if not its sound, however that is measured (voiced) by the one called "reader." And how else does the poem get read except in the hearing of it. (Listening to reading frames the poem in terms of one's experience of hearing it read.) The poem's literal information, that is, as notes in music, determines the shape ("shape") of what's heard. To paraphrase Olson/Creeley, *sound is never more than an extension of shape*—its shape being in the poem a matter of the line and how whatever syntax is there unravels itself along it.

It's not that semantic meaning in a poem doesn't matter, nor that poetry matters primarily as sound apart from meaning. Rather, the poet's act of composition—and reader/listener's performance of that composition, whether as written (seen) visual text or spoken (heard) acoustic text—involves the physical presence of words and the spaces between words whose identity is a matter of shape and sound. Our experience of shape and sound, what we see on the page and hear in the air (eyes vs. ears: perception of print vs. perception of pitch, accent, duration, etc.) makes possible *any* experience of a text's meaning. Poets "do" things with words, as do readers and listeners, both acts grounded in the fact that words are themselves "things," "objects," "material," "phenomena" as such. The shapes of letters in words and the music of those shapes read aloud are intimately engaged in the production of lexical meaning, which is itself different from yet inextricably bound to whatever any poem can be said or thought to "mean."

Think of the long line currently being explored by Mei-mei Berssenbrugge (and others), a line whose shape plays a particular music (and meaning) that wouldn't come about by any other means:

> *As far as the transparency or relative compression of her boundaries is concerned, and your backward focus to it:*
>
> *A white glass of wat er is hard to conceive of, because we cannot depict how the same thing would be white and clear, and how this would look. She doesn't know what description these words demand of her, since she is alone.*
>
> *She can sometimes see the events of a story as if they lay behind a screen, and it were transparent, rather like a sheet of glass, since human beings can be reflected*

> *on a smooth white surface in such a way that their reflections seem to lie behind the surface, and in a certain sense are seen through it.*

One is compelled to go forward here, at a pace commensurate with the speed the eye can cross the page, taking in such "content" as may be available, though that is not "the point" of such writing. Where it is going in the time it takes to get there is the sound it makes, in words that make the world in its own sound (shape) as thought.

If the sentence stops (at the period) there is a break (in sound), during which *Beautiful, unrepeatable, fleeting impressions can be framed . . .* [as] *a way of repeating a dream.* Which is to say, thinking now of Stein, the time *of* the poem ("composition") and time *in* the poem ("composition") are precisely the same, at least in the act of reading (sounding).[1]

To speak of the junction between two thoughts is necessarily to distort the fluidity of thinking, whose sound is inevitably continuous—no bars, no gaps, a single measure equal to the person's life. What appears to be different is only the next ph(r)ase in the curve "beginning again and again."[2]

> *You can be trying to connect the experience of being lost with something external or physical, but we are really connecting what is experienced with what is experienced.*

The connection of "this" to "this" becomes apparent as the shape (along horizontal and vertical notational axes—pitch, duration, "silence") of the poem's sounds, this one and that: "And after that what changes what changes after that, after that what changes and what changes after that and after that and what changes and after that and what changes after that."[3]

The longer the line the further it glides, its gesture (shape—sound—meaning) to this extent determined by punctuation, which pauses, and the line break itself, which frames syntax at the margin (edge) of thought.

> *Anything with limits can be imagined, correctly or incorrectly, as an object,*
> *even some language in the way that it is remembered, if you consider*
> *each repetition a fact or object of varying strength in various situations of*
> *frequency and quantity.*

Seeing (hearing) the shape (sound) of the poem, one discovers what it means to say: "the sound and pitch emphasis of a word are never apart from its meaning."[4] *To deny this is to deny the struggle to make certain meanings stick.*

What the sound of the poem contributes to its meaning is everything that matters. In such an event (in time) the sound of the text fills the page (air). *Because your eye clings to this margin, it appears to speed up.* As Alan Davies has written, "The moment's attention, locked to any sound from inside any word:— that structure must locate itself from within and without, in relation to such points."[5]

When Zukofsky defined the poem as "a context associated with 'musical' shape, musical with quotation marks since it is not of notes as music, but of words more variable than variables, and used outside as well as within the context with communicative reference," he means

> *The speaking* [poem] *is a constant notation of parallel streams of thought and observations*
> *whose substance is being questioned in a kind of oral thought at once open and precise.*

Likewise, his attempts to locate the poem in terms of its "limits" ("upper limit music, lower limit speech"; "poetry may be defined as an order of words that as movement and tone [rhythm and pitch] approaches in varying degrees the wordless art of music as a kind of mathematical limit") mean to think of a structure (of sounds) which, until read, "convey[s] the totality of perfect rest." Setting the poem's words into the air, *to be a spontaneous part of the desire itself, where coincidence and nonsense merge,* is to release (sound) the potential held in its body (shape); as Zukofsky again puts it, "The feelings of painting and sculpture travel with the movement; the body of what is seen is in the music."[6]

Writing the poem is this act: an extension (placement) of words from the body. *The route-through tightens around the nervous system like a musculature.* One feels (finds) the words, touching the page.

To say it again, the sound of the words: the rhythm of the body. And if words are to the poem as notes to a musical score, the person who "plays" the poem becomes "the instrument of language. The writer has written the writer,"[7] who thereby acquires *the power to make the space continue beyond the single perception, into raw material or youth of the body, like a body of light.*

The poem is the sound whose meaning (heard) is the sound of the poem

> *dissolv*[ing] *now at the top of her head, now five lights into her heart. Now, it dissolves into her body. Her friends dissolve into light. They dissolve into her family, which seems to dissolve into clouds that were already full of light.*

The words on the page (in the air, then ear) "do" nothing but this.

Zukofsky, again, quoting Stevens: "poetry [the body] is the subject of poetry [the body]."[8] What is to be said (written) will be heard by listening to the sound of thought, whose shape coincides with its meaning. Not the sonogram but sound itself, meaning its own identity—

for which a particular light can represent an initial condition. Even the slightest movement
of a hand or a finger is controlled and emphasized as by a spotlight of this sensitiveness,
the way repetition is a cessation of the potential for conscious experience.

The stopping of any thought, or turning at the line break, is a moment (temporary) of "silence," to be followed again *the way any moment that happened and in which you think about her goes / a long way toward convincing you of the autonomy and pre-existence of her form.* As John Cage has written,

"What we re-quire is
silence ; but what silence requires
is that I go on talking ."[9]

Cage (again):

"What I am calling poetry is often called content.
I myself have called it form . It is the conti-
nuity of a piece of music."[10]

The one who reads (hears) becomes the one who writes to the extent that she imagines the continuity of that sound. Such an act of imagination, as Adorno points out (paraphrasing Stockhausen), "is the passage of the work through the subject, is not some fixed quantity but a variable,"[11] depending for instance on the person.

She is not the name of a person, nor there *of a place, but they are connected with names.*
There is a way of traveling, by rotating an orientation, while she remains within herself.

Her existence takes place in the poem, whose words are the sound (meaning) of the world (knowledge) she thinks she knows. Communication between writer and reader (listener), as Cage writes, "takes place of its own/ accord,/ is/ for all the world/ inevitable."[12]

Writing, then, is the sound the reader shapes, listening. The moment the poem is sounded

is the space of the point of a moment in your seeing him or hearing him.

You can calm yourself by moving toward one of these points, the way you move along your own breath.

The reading of the poem is its own thought, making sense by meaning shape (sound), *a body of a cloud, which shifts in and out of focus* as one reads oneself into consciousness. Of the world, in words, as shape towards sound—

> *This is the realm or field in which other people exist in subtler forms than the body in daylight. A part of the person can become visible at a time, or parts of the people, and other parts rest in folds of the fog, as if they were muffled sounds.*

Passages in italics are from *Empathy*, by Mei-mei Berssenbrugge (Barrytown, NY: Station Hill Press, 1989).

Eigner's "Scores"

In Larry Eigner's poems, words and spaces (on the page) present and represent time and space (in the world). His poems are physical "events," bodies whose parts (typed) "count": as lines recording (imagining) perceptions, divisions between lines the passage of time—

the force

crash of a car

accordion

streetlights

dimmer than day

they were burning all night

stars

it's raining

—the displacement of words a notational register of (f)acts, as if language ("here" [on the page]) could mark (map) geographic location:

in the shadow

cross

winds

sunlight

as if over "there," elsewhere.

One doesn't commonly find "I" in Larry Eigner, though plenty of "eye":—what sees what's around one being in his case primary. This is not because Eigner, who sits in his wheelchair and types his poems with one (right index) finger, has no dramatic emotional "story" to tell, as one might think. Rather, his interior life and dreams (re)play out—in or as or over—the day's events, as if to say *DOWN ON THE BED you/ can't/ imagine/ enough,* the fact of what takes place in absolutely present time being of continual interest to one who has his presence of attention (focus) to track it. And with that act of what amounts to a record of time's inexorable "passage," Eigner's mental and emotional (*and* physical) life transcribes itself into these shapes:

the

frosted car

I imagine

hearing the motor

of the girl who lives here

or next door

upstairs

now

the snow heavy

hours

such days

that's it

news

what

drives away

the world.

Where words move in falling (dropping) from top left margin down (across) the otherwise blank page takes one by surprise—that of knowing suddenly the next thought ("that's it/ news/ what/ drives away/ the world") may not be around forever.

There's a register of quiddity ("thisness," fact) as precisely as language can gauge it, where position (of words) and the rhythm of successive instances of that set down (record, invent, discover) all that may be pertinent. Being an eye has its point too, given that it can see—

open road

you look in houses

and the night sky

any place

is all one

this time

—mind attend. His poems are literally "meditations."

To read Eigner's poems on the page, one is confronted with the fact of "it": poem as object, the two-dimensional plane of the page a field in which words play themselves out, making sound:

another plane is
gas   far,   a lot,   the night

shadows too

the fish tank bubbles

everything stand

continue   shapes.

To *hear* Eigner's poems read aloud *in his own voice* (inaccessible to most listeners, those at least not used to his speaking habit) is to come face to face with the power of words to convey sense by sound (alone). For if one cannot "understand" Eigner speaking his poems—cannot make out what the words are—one nonetheless hears what is essential: pace, tone, pitch, pause, silence read (pronounced) according to the poem's (page's) direction. Given that each person who speaks is a fraction of the world's community of speakers, in terms of numbers (this street, neighborhood, town, county, region), there is always the possibility that one will not be "understood." Eigner's poems (scores) represent in notational form the sounds of a voice that otherwise would not be heard. What is heard, according to the poem's directions for reading it, is a record of what is seen (perception), shaped not only to remember and preserve but to enact and imagine "it" into existence:

the sound

sea through the horizon
under the stand of trees

it comes by on the wind

flat and round
earth and sky.

Knowing the moment in such terms, one is conscious: something is alive, it exists, is blessed.

flock of birds
a moment
of one tree reached

apples fall to the ground

Passages in italics are from *Waters/ Places/ A Time* (Santa Barbara, CA: Black Sparrow Press, 1983).

Idea's Mirror

I. *writing ghost writing*

What happens when history enters the work the poet makes as if that work and history were images of one another, synonymous, the poet (present, subjective) and history (past, an "object" one knows of through other written texts) coincident insofar as the one takes the other's "facts" as somehow reflective, assumes its otherness to mark out the interior currents one's life unfolds daily, from time to time? Out the window the light advances down the eastward-facing hill the run rises to *STay Passenger/ BEhold a Mirror* one calls necessarily distant, say, the *King's Book* released the day Charles I of England lost his head on the scaffold outside the Banqueting House at Whitehall, London, 30 January 1649. One thinks of the past precisely as past, until that is *The Author of the Fact* in what must be construed as truly a leap—across time, of faith, *A pivot thrown on this person*—discovers a language in whose pastness one's own perceptions, present feelings, *at times at times* lie waiting to be brought forward to the reader who would bear (meaning) with them, piece together the signs of that life's correspondences to what has occurred "otherwise" as *torn among fragments/ Emblems gold and lead.*

When Susan Howe (re)writes the words she finds in Edward Almack's *A Bibliography of the King's Book; or, Eikon Basilike* (London, 1896), a copy of which she tells us her son found at a book sale of "useless books" at the Sterling Memorial Library at Yale, she means for the issues raised to be seen and heard as hers: What is the source of writing? What happens to it when it goes where it goes? In what sense does the person who happens to have been "the author" live in the words that "live" (where? in what circumstance?) after she or he has disappeared? Moreover, given that language itself unfolds a life of its own, one whose family branches extend "backward" in time from whatever present tense we find ourselves about to write, using words others have likewise used before, what work is ever entirely, unequivocably "new": *Was there ever an original poem? What is a pure text invented by an author? Is such a conception possible* whether or not what we write to find out what we don't know of ourselves, our world, stands *the test of time, the timeliness of libraries* on whose shelves others' "useful" books remain to show us *to* them, their world, a *Historiography of open fields* in whose pitch and spread I am predicated, reminded of myself the moment I open the book to read a *Language of state secrets,* a person who *bowed down his voice and said/ two or three words/ in a low voice* whose echo sounds off *the wall the brazen wall* he faced, faces again as I face the page, read the words that break the air's nearly perfect sense?

Somewhere it is true there were *Steps between Prison and Grave a Brazen Wall,* a moated grange, a *form of figure of thought* at first/last thought best repeated. When Howe quotes Sir Thomas More's *And so they said that these matters be Kynges games, as it were stage playes, and for the most part plaied vpon scafoldes,* she looks back to him looking forward not only to Charles on the block to lose his head at Whitehall but Howe at her desk to find hers in Guilford, Connecticut. *For the Author lies in his Gaol/ and knows not why,* whether it be the physical walls of a prison or, by the *small trespass to misprision* Howe sets forward to show us how attention—to fact, to the detail *Left scattered in disguise* one finds everywhere revealed—shows us the things of the world we didn't know we knew, the walls of her head *at home in my library/ I will lie down to sleep.* In a text that moves without warning from the language of 1989 to the language of 1649, *she/ was/ winding/ wool// Cloud/ soft/ threada/ twist,* each measure of her sense of what it means to be breathing in the world *This word* Remember. For this is a book in whose memory the fact of memory sets itself down to work upon the reader the telepathy of language *Disembodied beyond language,* a sense Howe makes present *Arriving on the stage of history I saw madness of the world* surrounding her, them, then, now.

She is gone she sends her memory, then, as if to say what I see now arrives through the lens as mirror I looked through to find my own image. *I feared the fall of my child/ resting quietly with some hopes/ as a bird before any* sense that it will sing or fly from the branch where it does so, unseen. Hardly the name, for in *Saying so I name nobody* you know, save that Howe with acknowledgment of the help of others writes *In his Pseudomisus/ shifts the balance/ of emphasis* from what might be merely the "personal," private self at public wall to that wider context that sees the continuities linking her and them to us. *She is the blank page/ writing ghost writing,* hers the *Night page torn word missing/ The family silence/ gave up the ghost, her remains of light blue silk/ strings*—her book ours to do with as we please, which will be to carry us forward into a world coincident at every point with what was and is, for each of us, *IN | HIS | SOLITUDE* all ways, completely present.

Passages in italics are from *A Bibliography of the King's Book; or, Eikon Basilike* (Providence, RI: Paradigm Press, 1989; rpt. *Singularities* [Hanover, VT and London: Wesleyan University Press, 1990]).

II.

Words for Susan Howe are what count when the pulse that fills the body fails. Her world is distant, a *coherent rational system* save that it would be discovered in the space articulation makes for it, on the page, between lines the *same and not the same,* tracing history's revenge, speaking as quickly as shifting turns toward the sun's *gossamer* (abyss) *kinsmen trespass.* One looks back to one's place in the rooted *escaping conclusion,* Amherst *millstones/ Sleep* rounded with a little of something taken in focus turned backward, up a notch to an aperture fixed at ASA 400 even the woman in the dark would read: this no mere feminine *theoreticians of the Modern* claiming themes of silence and speech, but *rational and supernatural* calls to power at the center of the room.

What this writing adds to and up to *depends on memory,* the poet idea's *mirror, a transcriber* of the real known to be moving across the screen of vision, not only voice but sight sound taste smell touches in the brain *emblematical* of the girl on the porch dressed in black who is flying backward into her fantasy of what was and is the imagined life. A pencil might hold *'Farewell' left in a sentence* were it not otherwise humanistic, the discipline violently *Antecedent terror stretched to a whisper* organicism hears twitching its paw on the table. Not that someone *raised in a strict evangelical household* could for a moment not think, not notice the scant juncture each precept leads perception to fill an instant ahead of such time *story* sees to be told *beyond any book* thus written, this writing *hierarchies suggest* will take its place in a discourse sentiment takes to the field, feeling that whenever the candle burns another can be found asking *the light, mock light?*

That will be silence *we that were wood,* active in work to make sense *a hunter's gun,* seriousness *from what she thought was a panther,* was a note the tune played once, wasn't forgotten *exactly equivalent* to how a syntax forced the relation of part to part, part to whole *Posit gaze* when measure could say be there in the rhythm of words forward *step shot Immanence force* and back *sideup*

upside turning attention *essentially anonymous,* not an author to display self at any cost, prize, hers if one were to choose *Master. Hope* programs the circle the arrows back against, hand drawn figure jamming *wanton meteor ensign streaming* through the galaxy behind our eyes to make sure what we think thinks itself too.

As Howe speaks the language *grasps its subject/ stumbling phenomenology* what we find when the gun, loaded, goes off. Hers in the silence the space between words and lines announces whenever *I lay down and conceive,* the sound (*her cry// silences// whole// vocabularies// of* names// *for* things. Say we do live in the finite world in Boston, say, that place good as any *ticked perfectly* to those our predecessors called theirs, these words making way *into the immediate* feeling *of understanding.* Sometimes as usual adjective preceding the noun, *deaf evening* hears the cement contract in the joints of words, *mother heaved higher* to see her one child the one of many who cross the porch into the dark, the *infinite miscalculation of history* not merely what criticism can hope to call its own but more, the ghost of the one—*beneath the hill—/ whose service*—we take to heart aiming the gun *linked time and again* to looking to where the patterns meet. *rhymed order* carries it through the sound the words meet *blowing Edgar's mad song.* We keep up pretext of her text, knowing as much as fast as she alouds.

The connections meet as soon as letters across the expanse between words collide. Collage isn't only part, the whole of it bound by what *root casket tangled scrawl* makes us perceive as we read the message these words encode, breaking silence. What is left after that contact *More than language can express* stands for all she knows the reader knows. To meet her there at the point of *sense into empty// Thread gone* will be of a sufficiency beyond simple perusal of type set in a book in Windsor, say, Vermont *shrinking back to dark.* If the universe is physical to us, as indeed we only must guess it, then this is a body as *time in the center of a room/ doubt is spun* only every day in taking the next step after the last, lost.

Silence as a theme arcs across the gap sound leaves, moving away. *sense gathers moss* the longer it goes untended, she whose foot would tread the measure a gate suggests limited to access in so far as orthography changes *to faint slaughter story so. This surface scission is deceptive,* as it was for her ancestors Dickinson and Stein, who *meet each other along paths of the Self* one finds here *tense/ as an outsider.* (Re)Arrangement of the past(time) is not in her view idle play but a pleasure whose end means the present won't go without notice. *Out of America's text free past, sounds spelled* Kain-tuck-kee *are an Indian place.* So she names the heroes Boone, Finley, Cooper, Mather, Edwards, Webster, Thoreau. Later and elsewhere others called Beach, Weaver, *Zukofsky near the end of* Bottom: on Shakespeare.

If they be two, they are two so
As stiffe twin compasses are two,

how *A lyric poet hunts after some still unmutilated musical wild of the Mind's world.* Because it isn't as if we won't get it if she doesn't give it up, or over, through the notes the words note, but that if one can say exactly the version she herself maintains along lines extending toward the horizon, from beyond which the front whose clouds now pass over us has approached. Later the *time of sleep memory dreams* will turn upon itself, and find in this direction its own way, the one *awake guarding the Distance.*

Once the frontier, now words map a way into what we only thought we knew, discovering territory bounded by *Ridges of sand rising on one another// Mathematics of continua* like the cup of hot milk she takes before bed as ritual, *Rhythm and Pedestal// Room of dim.* Whoever comes to the door may knock, ring, stamp her presence altogether certain—*under the old misappellation*—that what can be said will now be, as if once the tree among others falls no one who isn't there hears a thing *cry a cause/ (no lie).* Spacing themselves the words *interpret flame.* She writes belief as if what the potential a reader will find there matters, counts itself chosen to stay. Those referred to articulate the history that even now presides, making present know the way it came to be herein state. *alone, in her clearing of Becoming,* Howe proves what has been contemporaneous to what is, given what follows springs from roots as *milk runs in the breast of each mother* close enough to hear the sound forms.

And so we take the book to heart, *Out among haphazard children// sunny investigations of Permanence* marking a trial whose judge and witness constitute the mind so engaged it sees itself in the other, hears what calls *Time comprehended in Thought* as lines in columns of words becoming a *figure moving in color,* fainting the fragments poetry would keep the world whole by. Her conviction stuns an audience unused to knowing how serious turns of thinking might go, yet nearly all delight inhabits here. We come from this changed, having taken in that which invites the interpenetration of fixed frames of sense heretofore known if at all as one's *face of blank force,* the name you carry after the tape stops. Setting forward then into the field, where *coveys nestle and settle// Meditation of a world's vast Memory* proves the aim as much as any can be to take, this writing test indeed of the rock words can build upon and have, *pitched across history,* inventing the world *skiff feather glide house.*

Passages in italics are from *Articulation of Sound Forms in Time* (Windsor, VT: Awede, 1987; reprinted in *Singularities* [Hanover, VT and London: Wesleyan University Press, 1990]), *My Emily Dickinson* (Berkeley: North Atlantic Books, 1985), and *Pythagorean Silence* (New York: Montemora, 1982; reprinted in *The Europe of Trusts* [Los Angeles: Sun & Moon Press, 1990]).

Utter Mimesis

Michael Davidson's *Analogy of the Ion* investigates the nature of the written world—how writing presents its failure to represent the world it writes. The book's epigraph from Kierkegaard ("If the world, instead of being beauty, were nothing but equally large unvariegated boulders, there would still be no repetition"), which questions the very possibility of (re)presentation, suggests its concern with what might be called the "principle of rhyme," according to which identities unified by a strong but strongly imperfect likeness pull simultaneously together and apart, and its eight-part structure (composed of two pairs of opening and closing sections of prose sentences, which frame a pair of inner sections whose poems literally mirror one another and themselves frames a pair of center sections composed of Davidson's analogy of Plato's *Ion* together with his commentary on Plato/Davidson's dialogue) itself illustrates the physics of that principle. What exactly is the relation between the world as we know it and any representation (i.e., "repetition") of that world? Does A in fact ever equal A'? the event its history? the person her story? the place a painter's view of it or writer's description? And in what sense does experience of the world translate into the literal substance of its retelling, as representation of concrete fact becomes words that signal, for instance, "the rain begins to strike the roof"—a sentence whose properties (including sound), no matter how evocative, do not include (real) water striking (real) shingles?

The incapacity of language to represent any thing, person, place, event, thought, feeling, or perception has to do with the fact that writing constructs not the world itself but its own world of words, creating for the reader or listener a potential experience *of words* suggestive of, but never exactly equivalent to, any actual experience in the world. The equivocal nature of the contract may be seen in the following sentences, each of which appears to undermine or counteract the statement it appears to be making:

> *Up there in Sonoma, down in L.A., back in the Midwest, out in Wyoming she studies the law where jurisdiction does not occur in the same place twice.*
>
> *The circle is the house is the measure is the map is the sky.*
>
> *They became friends of mimesis, each referring to himself by the other's name.*
>
> *In between the first and second descriptions a tense had changed even though both refer to the same event.*
>
> *They showed us the photograph of the miniature city modelled on the actual city in which they had stayed which included a perfect replica of the miniature city within the miniature city and so forth.*
>
> *He is unclear whether the first time he saw his father was in the living room or in the photograph of the living room in which his father appeared in uniform.*

> *"I made her so mad she was burning" caused her to understand "she was burning" she was so mad.*
>
> *A tree-like grid imposed itself upon the actual tree, allowing him to understand an architecture the leaves obscure.*
>
> *The letter contained references to persons now scattered about the landscape who are at this point and by displacement largely textual and from henceforth will be known as A, B, C, et cetera.*
>
> *Many of the missing details could be obtained by phoning the individuals in question who invariably contradicted what others had said earlier history is a perpetual phonecall.*

Any of one's perceptions may spark the impulse that moves one to record in writing that perception, but the slippage between words, and even larger gap between words and world, works in effect to sabotage one's attempt to translate actual perception into language. Words, whose own structures and dynamics inevitably take hold whenever one speaks or writes, tend to take over, as if moved by impulse of their own: *He wrote out of desire to stand over history, one foot in the Adriatic and the other in the Lago di Garda, while soldiers made their way up treacherous mountains of typographical errors and lacunae.* Timing is everything tense claims (*Epos is not cold history he wrote slash he writes; Once it was new and then it became time*), grammar as central to our self-awareness and knowledge of the world at large as sight, hearing, touch, taste, smell: *Had he been wasting his time making empty statements of fact was the only way he could frame his discomfiture over the absence of interrogatives.* So we recognize in the multiple and accidental intersections between language and the world that any sentence may distort the "truth" (*They had contrived a solution to the problem of the homeless by reinterpreting their plight as a need to assert their freedom to choose not to come indoors*); may be the result of forces outside it we can't identify (*Only the measure of squirrels moving across the roof controls the deployment of his phrases*); may be subject to any and all kinds of "system errors" (*You can erase these mistakes with ease became you can erase these mistakes with ease*); and therefore may well be mistaken (*What he meant by A at that early date was not what he meant now he was at pains to point out in a series of published disclaimers*).

Davidson explores this capacity of language for "failure"—its inherent urge to bend, twist, shade, slant, miscast, and color what it talks about, and its consequent inability to "represent" (i.e., repeat)—most directly in sections 3 and 6 of *Analogy of the Ion,* which systematically mirror one another, in that each of the forty-two lines of the poem in section 3 is "answered" by a line in section 6:

If plus heat	*Then fog minus hills*
three as three	*four as before or*
a man marked man . . .	*woman marked man . . .*

Each poem stands independently of its mate, of course, as one's first reading of section 3 clearly insists, but each is also drawn across the space filled by sections 4 and 5, depending upon this "missing" identity the other supplies in order to complete itself.

Declaring in effect the utterly equivocal face of language, each identity in this concentric mirrorlike structure of poems is mimed by—"rhymes" with—its twin, a parallel or opposite or consequent identity in the other poem. It's as if the fabric of one poem turns literally inside out in the other, *plus* followed by *minus, ice tray* by *fire pan, and makes small talk* by *but elaborates:*

he writes at desk	*she fingers knife*
the Denver Tosca	*the Dallas Norma*
up here out there	*up there out here*
was patient even	*will approach odd*
birds on deck	*absence of birds in*
I quit . . .	*you begin . . .*

and so on and on, to *this last* *that first.*

The "repetition" as echo made explicit here in the large and small-scale structure of *Analogy of the Ion* implies a perception about the world and the ability of words to encompass it. Analogy, from the Greek *análogos* ("proportionate") suggests not only the partial similarity of any two related identities but the absolutely essential separation that makes each term of any pair unique. A doesn't repeat A' no matter how close we bring them toward one another, no matter how carefully we attempt to "say" A with A'. Balancing at its center, as if to demonstrate within the framework of other cases in point exactly how writing both does and does not repeat, section 4 of *Analogy of the Ion* presents a re-writing of Plato's dialogue *Ion,* in which Socrates proves to the naive rhapsode-poet Ion that poetry isn't art but inspiration given by the gods, that a poet *is a light and winged thing, and holy, and never able to compose until he has become inspired, and is beside himself, and reason is no longer in him.* In showing that poets don't have the specific useful knowledge of the world that doctors or horsemen or generals have, Plato aims to discredit poets, whom he elsewhere casts out of his Republic for telling "lies," making only "copies" of the truth. Similarly, in following the argument of the dialogue even as he reduces it to an often streetsmart urban slang—

Ion: *And so we reciters read the readers, if I read you right.*
Sokrates: *Right, I figures you'd come round. But wait . . . let's say you're saying some Homer one Tuesday, and you come to the part where Odysseus unmasks himself before the suitors. You know the part?*

—Davidson invites us to reexamine not only Plato's attack on poets, who *like Proteus . . . twist and turn, this way and that, assuming every shape . . . in order to deceive* but also the sacredness of Plato's (or any) text.

For any text is a reading of some prior text(s), some whole string of writings that in coming after it can't help but echo, comment upon, and change. So Davidson's little dialogue is itself followed by a series of pseudo-critical remarks, in which Plato/Davidson talks about his work and the issues it raises:

> *In other dialogues I've argued that poets corrupt the morality of the State, but here, for the sake of argument, I claim that the only good poet is one who knows what he's talking about. Ion may be a good reciter of Homer, but he doesn't know much about poetry—precisely because there's nothing there to know. Poetry is a simulacrum of everything everyone has said already and to repeat is only to validate this very fact.*

So what one says, so Michael Davidson says in his poem "Utter Mimesis," which stands outside of but adjacent to the concerns of *Analogy of the Ion, becomes more than a mirror.* Writing doesn't repeat the world but creates in the dynamics of its multiple structures an analogue of the world and of its effect upon us: *Paper over stone creates scissors, scissors cut stone into rocks you throw them at teachers, passers by, you could also write them and achieve the same effect.* And if that world and its effect may at times be beautiful, as Kierkegaard and poets since before Plato have recognized, Davidson's work shows us that our perception of that beauty, and indeed the common denominator of all aesthetic pleasure, involves the discovery of what we don't know in what we do: *Poetry lifts the veil from the hidden beauty of the world and makes familiar objects be as if they were not familiar.*

Passages in italics are from *Analogy of the Ion* (Great Barrington, MA: The Figures, 1988; reprinted in *Post Hoc* [Bolinas, CA: Avenue B, 1990]).

Writing *A Reading*

Her epigraph from George Steiner's *After Babel* suggests that Beverly Dahlen's *A Reading 1–7* is conceived of as an "open" or "interminable" work, one without boundaries or end: "Wittgenstein asked where, when, and by what rationally established criterion the process of free yet potentially linked and significant association in psychoanalysis could be said to have a stop. An exercise in 'total reading' is also potentially unending."

The words move forward in *writing I was sitting there the cat and the light saw it for the first time,* as thinking of words (in words) can or will make what one knows become the knowledge that language (itself) calls its own. Dahlen, writing it, sounds the space of language itself, as Rachel Blau DuPlessis suggests in her statement on the back cover:

> Reading "it"—the unknown, the unconscious, the past, the language, woman—by endless invention of "it." A writing/ a reading: a physical and mental labor to create the endless tissue and fissure of meditation, (one's) time, place, mind, pulse; processual, resistant, desirous. A stunning, cunning and canny, an *un*canny work.

A Reading is writing the reader happens to come upon in the world (of "things," that is "events") represented on the page by words *stopping on the word it turns around.* It is meaning to explore *the person or god who made it,* the present and (mythic) past *in which everything speaks* in a language that measures the relation between writer and reader, *another code, another order, a counter order, the question of loving strange women, what that should be necessary, universally, the necessity of loving strange women.* From each instant of the reading will emerge the future, a form of consciousness itself surrounded by what is not known (the unconscious), the discovery of which (here) *is like hacking one's way through an impenetrable jungle only to come at once upon a precipice beyond which is an unfathomable drop. It is a moment of absolute lucidity joined with absolute ignorance.*

In writing the (unending) text of one's life, one thinks to know what is taken as fact. One is sitting on or in or beside or next to or with or across from the person who holds her chin in her hand. As soon as she begins, the reader listens to the voice that rides as if in the left lane of the freeway. As the car reflects the personality of its driver, her "view" (the woman's, the person's "view") is the person in the throes of (dis)figuring the one whose face had been struck by the windshield in the oncoming car, *too far away to think it was anyone else but me.* Does she react (does the radio work) when she comes to the door in her bathrobe after a night of interrupted sleep?

The voice one hears in *A Reading* goes on (*and on*), private as much as public, fragmented and coherent, subconscious and fully awake, anterior (interior) to the individual who is *what* [one] *knows, what mind, the double is with us till we die,* fully present, right here, now. It is a voice, as Robert Duncan wrote of Dahlen's *Egyptian Poems,* that "comes from 'below'—a speech below speech." *this was a kind of writing. of speech. tonguing,* as she herself has written.

Hers is a writing that, reflecting her life in the world, inevitably reflects upon itself (as reading), tests the capacity of language to "mean" in ways one ordinarily expects. Her *text mimics speech, a talk, imagining you, the second person, or persons, others to whom I speak in the future, the end of October, the darkness rising.* When we read it (or hear it read) we comprehend by listening to her (private) life broadcast so to speak in these words, made present (play-by-play) *because the words take the place of another.* The reader is as much responsible (for meaning, to meaning) as the one who has written, because *the reading of the writing goes on . . . because you are not here. you are always not here, you are never here, I make you up, I wonder how you look. and now it is so much easier to write than to speak. an other is so much an hallucination it's scary. I don't know what I speak to.*

The writing is *A Reading* in the sense that it answers to one's need (to be spoken). The poem does not seek to bare one's soul but rather to discover (one's) meaning *and the simple story of its plot.* The narrative proceeds by means of recording what the mind thinks it thinks at any point. *she who pondered all these things silently* would not have written this poem.

The poem is an experiment in form, sound, syntax, visual shape as well as a rethinking of the (modernist) principles of image, narrative and personal voice, the *same in here and yet not the same/ losing its leaves and flowers.* The work is interesting in that it creates what is known (and not known) *here, because you are not here.* The person who is reading is *learning how to live in an artificial environment,* as is the one who has written *A Reading.*

It will be said that this book is not accessible, is difficult or resistant to interpretation. It will also be said that such writing makes no "difference," or that its "difference" is merely "gender-based" (woman's writing), "open" because it cannot be otherwise. The more accurate way of reading *A Reading* will recognize that what is difficult or different shows us the way we are (in words) and where (in the world) we are going. *the continuity had been shattered; she wondered why it had turned out this way. why in the world, expecting the end of it, it would continue, coming true.*

Passages in italics are from *A Reading 1–7* (San Francisco: Momo's Press, 1985).

Cracking the Code

For the listener, hearing David Bromige's "Indictable Suborners" for the first time is like finding yourself in the funhouse with unlimited access to all the rides: the hall of mirrors with air holes in the floor, the rollercoaster slides, the giant turntable that spins and spins until everyone but the one braced at the center slides off. It's fast and funny, each new sentence a surprise (*Jumping ahead—or somewhere, anyway—lands me on the square called Kierkegaard*), and with no discernable narrative continuity you settle back for the ride. And then, suddenly, you crack the code. That is, you begin to discover patterns in what at first seemed a barrage of ideationally unrelated (and unrelateable) sentences, sentences that often as not seem to hover somewhere between sense and nonsense, as in this representative passage, the poem's opening:

> *And hands comb some one annual rainfall in the silence after laughter in Brandenburg. In the unlikely event, lust for salvation woos the marginals, looking for some surrogate Sunday won't remove come Monday. Contemplative, one head high on an ash-heap is in a telegram by way of Hello from Doncaster. The recurrence tells itself over and over, it makes part of the instant, recognition. Event and clarity shake and make up in clear weather some little distance from the center of Fenwick. If we witness our world every evening from the remove of its circumference, how are we identical with ostlers in jodphurs when the iamb kept hoofing it along? Gluing frames of film together, an editor means to indicate either the passage of time or simultaneous occurrences in Hooverville.*

There are all sorts of local details of language working against the disparateness of these sentences, knitting the fabric together: *rainfall/clear weather/clarity, remove* (verb)/*remove* (noun), *event/Event, center/circumference, Sunday/Monday/the passage of time, hoofing/Hooverville.* (The fact that one doesn't notice such incidental rhymes in no way diminishes their presence, nor their effectiveness in creating the sort of casual and random patterning effects that operate throughout "Indictable Suborners": in a listener's or reader's experience of any work, unnoticed effects are more effective—and more valuable—than noticed ones.) There is also a systematic (though again at this point hardly perceptible) recurrence of place names that, as it continues, makes the poem something of a travelogue whose itinerary includes points on the map most of us not only haven't been to but probably haven't heard of: *Brandenburg, Doncaster, Fenwick, Hooverville, Jinnah, Licata, Potter's Valley, Redwood City, Vukovar, Shanghai, Zelenogradsk, Atwater, Cedar Rapids, Ethelbert,* and so on. The list goes on and on, insistently, arbitrarily, and yet not, for it is itself part of the poem's principal organizing structure, the pattern of a sequential linking of letters in the alphabet. Again, one doesn't notice what one doesn't notice, at least at first, that the work is determined methodically from a to b to c (*And . . . Brandenburg . . . Contemplative . . . Doncastor*

. . . Event . . . Fenwick . . . Gluing . . . Hooverville)—seven complete circuits through the alphabet (five in prose and two in verse, with an empty "analphabetic" sentence in the first four prose sections intervening between each of the sentences whose beginning and ending elements figure in the pattern), with a short verse coda at the end.

A reader who sees the poem in print will undoubtedly pick up its chief constructional device far more quickly than a listener who hears the poem read aloud. Most listeners, I imagine, would not discover it at all. When I heard Bromige read the poem in San Francisco on August 31, 1985, at what I believe was its "premier," it wasn't until the seventh section, where, without an intervening sentence, the distance between the linked letters shortens, that I was struck by the suddenly obvious concatenation:

> Visibly, *the trouble with this mode grows with every sentence; various it isn't, and for* why? Explanations *vary, but not much: the social I is hub to every spoke, within then a circumference, painted (why not)* yellow. Zero . . .

The question is not, in any case, who can piece together the evidence of a series of aural or visual clues, or under what circumstances the discovery of the overall pattern first occurs, but what those clues and the impulse behind them have to do with the poem and what else goes on in it.

The fact that "Indictable Suborners" is built upon an alphabetical pattern of repetition external to and independent of its substance—a pattern that is at once simple, mechanical, and completely predictable (and at one point at least implicitly referred to: *But all writing IS spelling, except for the illiterate oral traditional*)—suggests something important about that substance, by which I mean its ideational content as distinct from the formal structure it comes clothed in. That is, the substance of each new sentence unit, though it may simultaneously participate in the ongoing alphabetical scheme, is radically discontinuous from whatever precedes and follows it. This means that when we look at any extended passage from the poem we find two conflicting structural principles operating at once: the alphabetical matrix, which creates order within each whole section, and the local events of each sentence, whose randomness creates an equally urgent disorder of the parts within that whole. Here, for example, is the end of the third section, where the letters *t, u, v, w, x, y* and *z* work to bring closure in one system even though the sentences in which these letters occur have apparently nothing to do with closure, with each other, or with anything that has come before or after this passage:

> Tux *adjusted, the tenor hums under his breath ("Falling in lurv is jurst an infantile fahancy") preparatory to entertaining the human beings of a service club in* Uxbridge. *I sat for one hour, studying the candle burn down in the skull; then the lights came back on.* Verification *means the same in Paris as it means in* Wellington. *The translator, having weighed the conflicting demands of his task, remembered the word "version" and relieved his sigh of a heave.* Xenophobia *steadied the hand and aim of the follower of the bearded prophet in* Yemen. *The clear expression of mixed feelings was frequently what we were after.* Zero *either leads to further instances of itself, or back to the// beginning.*

With each sentence unit turning upon what Bromige calls at one point its own "*INTRICATE DELIGHTS,*" whatever and however incidental those may be (*THIS SENTENCE HAVING RESOLVED ITSELF AT THE OUTSET TO MAINTAIN UPPERCASE CONSISTENCY WHATEVER THE PROVOCATION DENIES ITSELF THE INTRICAIE DELIGHTS OF LITTLE A AND LITTLE G*), the poem invites us to turn full attention to the moment-by-moment events of language that constitute the text.

Some of those events occur in statements that sound like history with a twist (*Kicked out of bed for having a job, the farmhand attempted to murder his alarmclock in an attic in Licata*) or history condensed to the pithiness of a headline (*Rascals festoon maples with tp on Graduation Night in Saskatoon; Marmorial splendor for an alabaster episode*). And some lie in statements that sound like straightforward facts of life (*Three dried barleycorns = one inch, and a foot is a foot; The itchy patch on today's hand is yesterday's poison oak*) or not so straightforward facts of life (*For dinner tonight there will be ham and eggs in Gore; That clock so long in the family its ticking feels part of the home is a machine; Urine trickles down the leg of a person historically present in the intense preoccupation of a doorway in Voorst*). Much of the poem sounds like narrative, sometimes straightforward (*Next day she came back—why? He tapes their loudnesses of early morning [the power-saws, power-mowers, power-drills] and plays them back out the window with the volume all the way up at midnight*) but most often askew, either because of some trompe l'oeil effect of language (*Visible to no one, a beckoning youth winced with the iciness as he placed his other foot into the identical river one foot already stood in, near Wilderness Peak; Perhaps he had gone too far, mused an unmetaphorical fellow in [or no longer in] Quebec; Hints of the new burst into a linguistic atlas [alas] wearing winklepickers in Innishull*) or some bizarre twist of details which inevitably throws the story off:

> *Zebra-stripes distinguish these elegant models, studying to marry indolent to insolent, learning to manifest the hic of haeccity [sic] someplace downtown in an anonymous settlement in early Minoan// Aegea*
>
> *Ought the forms of thought be available to be bought, in their translucent pervasiveness, or ought . . . but the octogenarian trailed off into an instance of obliviousness in Port Moresby Nodding in the halflight (nodding at all), the ikons looked uncommonly tall, while a rat with a sail attached (how to enjoy one's cruelty and benefit humanity at the same time) to its tail looked to be wearing its master's toga, and the commemorative trees, under which it was once possible to holler and be heard, as if people could lengthen their arms by misspelling anatomy, and palms do wave in Odessa.*

Sometimes the narrative mode switches from third to first person, as in *Went to the mall and thought, these multi-valent voices are the brooks in William Wordsworth's books; came home and imagined Theodor Adorno catching Sebastian from "Brideshead Revisited" on "Love Boat" with two chimps in his bed.* In sentences like this, Bromige writes what sounds like straightforward autobiography, what he calls at one point in the poem *Autobiographical writing—"I go to the bank every Friday: On Fridays I go to the bank, and am pleased to observe that, since I complained about them to the metermaid, the phone company's trucks are no longer parked all day long on overdue city meters with orange cones in the street to confuse the citizenry of a place provincial enough to still care about such minor effects.* To represent his own life in thought in words as ordinary as these, Bromige states near the beginning of the poem (in a passage that also refers to going to the bank on Friday) *depends for its esthetic merit completely upon the perspicacity of the person, unless objective truth has meant for her liquidation in the sensation of a current event extraordinary enough to hypnotize anyone.* Objective truth in the world of this poem is highly problematic, subject as it is to Bromige's impulse to play with our expectations of coherence and continuity both within the sentence and from sentence to sentence, to explore words' capacity to shape, fracture, and discover the world.

In his essay "Some Fields the Track Goes Through," Bromige quotes Adorno on the virtues of "Irresponsible play," which "seeks to overcome the ruinous seriousness of whatever one happens to be."[1] Whether "seriousness" is in all cases "ruinous" I'm not sure, but it seems clear that there are no completely "serious" statements to be found in "Indictable Suborners," whose title itself suggests deception, secrecy, and outright lies. In another essay, on the distinction between poetry and philosophy, Bromige's account of his own use of deception in *Tight Corners & What's Around Them* (Los Angeles: Black Sparrow, 1974), offers a rationale for the playfulness in language we find here: "The tone is deliberately deceptive to remind a reader of the tricks we can (be) play(ed) (upon) with language. It reminds by putting one through the experience, as well as by indicating it."[2] One sentence, for example, literally puts us through the experience of a missing letter on the typewriter: *H was the key broken on her machine when she wrote that letter (I've been c atting about the roug ed-in in t inking wis ing I weren't so ampered by t ese tig ts on my t ig s) I found quite intriguing.* In another, an overabundance of abstract language does to a reader/listener what it does to the poor *cogitator in Mogadouro* whose story it presents:

> *Logically fallacious, the argument that an indeterminancy principle implies the existence of a specific value of a dynamic variable for a physical system whose quantum state is not an eigenstate of the hypermaximal Hermitean operator representing this variable in the formalism of the theory swayed a cogitator in Mogadouro.*

But as its title suggests, each sentence in "Indictable Suborners" is itself literally a "suborner"—a false witness whose playful deceptions invite us to experience the delights of ordinary (and extraordinary) language bursting its seams. Thus, *Sanskrit says he did going not he went; you're the one who goes not you will go; the breeze blew a book shut not he lost his place in Tanglewood.* Is this true? The first two assertions sound as though they might be, although at this point in the poem I doubt any reader could be expected to take them at face value, and losing one's place in Tanglewood simply blows the whole thing out of the tub. If it isn't true, why pay attention, why should we care? This is a real question, the answer to which, though simple, deserves some note. We care about how Sanskrit renders ordinary statements in English because the translation—given that it occurs in this text—is bound to be unpredictable, shocking, and fun. It is also bound to trace some thread of sense through whatever short circuit it leads us (when the book shuts one loses one's place), to discover a pattern of meaning outside the range we might have thought possible in this instance.

Bromige's remarks in an essay on the work of Clark Coolidge are relevant here: "CC, writing, is lost/found in his child's play, rearranging his magic objects until a pattern (on the instant become *the* pattern) creates . . . a sufficiency."[3] For in each sentence of "Indictable Suborners" there is some sort of pattern—"on the instant become *the* pattern," since every sentence operates independently of every other sentence despite each sentence's cooperation in the alphabetical system of the whole—which gives a separate and intrinsic identity to that sentence, and so provides it with a "sufficiency" compelling enough to give it its place in the whole. Certain of these patterns have simply to do with a structure of sound (*He hissed* this *at the geese crossing the barnyard in Iseltwald; Lissome lovelies hoist Mooseheads in Missoula*). Others are built upon parodic echo, as in *But what does not change could prove the will to change the topography of Cutknife* (Olson) or *the other mums (fret not in their narrow British shops)* (Wordsworth). Still others rely upon repetition, which Bromige at one point says is *practically redundant—moved by an elan vital (Eileen Vitale) far more (farmor) basic than knowing, flotsam in an unceasing, continuous, undivided (practically redundant) process—* but which most often discover some inner necessity for almost saying over what has just been said. Consider for example the ostentatiously insistent pattern of repetition in *Finally (finally [finally]), continuity at last (at last [ditto]) found (located [discovered]) asylum (refuge [shelter]) in ([no] wiser for its arrival) Geyserville*—a sentence that investigates random "continuity" by setting forth a three-part echo that shifts gradually across the space of the sentence, from exact replication of the leading term in *Finally,* to partial (but ideationally exact) replication in *at last (at last [ditto],* to repetition of idea by means of synonyms in *found (located [discovered]),* to instances where the pattern repeats itself not by words but marks of punctuation, in the parentheses *([no] wiser for its arrival).* So also we find in another sentence that a reiteration of certain random phrases with their word order randomly scrambled has the effect of putting one through the experience of having it both ways at once: *Everybody who is anybody (anybody who is everybody) who has eyes to see (who has to see eyes) and money to travel can study some figure of justice (and justice to study can travel some figure of money), but why be so agreeable?*

Within the matrix of alphabetically linked letters that gives "Indictable Suborners" its overall structural unity, Bromige asserts an aesthetic of randomness by enacting it in local events of language such as these. In writing a work of narrative discontinuity, he opens his hand, abandoning himself to the intricacies of whatever content was present at the moment of its writing. The world enters the work at every point—as complexity and measure and form—and its infinite variety is in turn mirrored and measured and shaped by the words given to the poet to present it. Bromige himself suggests as much in the essay on Coolidge: "The content it ["Weathers"] offers as its evidence could be, theoretically, anything—although in practice can't be but what CC happens, projectively, upon" (215). As in computer-generated fractals, where the reduplication of triangles in a pattern on a screen together with the random shifting of the positions of their vertices can create a three-dimensional illusion of space (Mount Whitney in the Sierra Nevada, say, as easily as craters on the moon), the multiplication of random events in the sentences that make up "Indictable Suborners" in effect brings the raw material of the poet's life onto the screen of the page, there to be decoded by the reader/listener. Moreover, the work demands from both poet and reader/listener the same stance of openness toward its words; as Bromige says in his essay on poetry and philosophy, "One may not stand above the words, commanding them to mean what one would have them mean, but instead has to exist among them, granting them their autonomous polysemy, their gratuitous capacities" (20). In allowing the accidents of language—these "gratuitous capacities" of its words—to enter the work and operate freely within its preconceptualized alphabetical scheme, Bromige calls attention to the random and essentially accidental nature of everyday life. *But by what argument banish the arbitrary and accidental from our councils? Denounced by the post Hegelian Kierkegaard, these elements nevertheless inform all events.* And it is just this power of accident in language to inform events that "Indictable Suborners" aims most to present, making clear the degree to which words can err *and* mirror, and so help make strange *and* intelligible, the world.

Passages in italics are from "Indictable Suborners" (unpublished manuscript).

Reading *Sun*

Reading Michael Palmer's *Sun,* meaning here *both speaking/not speaking,* one thinks, filling in the gaps behind words after the front (weather) has moved through, *Your English I do not speak. No buildings* hold the light long, facing north in winter, a morning the sky without a cloud appears *on looking out from this house* an isolate line of rooftops that make up city hillscape, *blue seven like this/ hazed* sometimes in winter though not this day.

A syntax emerges from the corner of the page, *the image of a child on a hill,* say, as if out of history ideas could spring fully formed yet in fragments, discrete, discreet, *freeze dried* the moment the poet *is ours, no part of this page* able to say precisely what it intends to fill the gaps with. *Call it Live* word music, simply put the street permits *(you cannot say things)* an occasion for reflection the sentence entertains as it moves *under the tongue,* direction inward *as it coats our skins* with an impulse—call it "lyric," call it "meditate," call it "*Sun,*" meaning here *Glides and rests—as inside the inside once* signals to the reader "I am here, hear me." *signed The World As It Is.*

A breeze the open window curtains moves *can see into the past through a lens.* An echo it is French to say who will or will not repeat with variation the substance, *a visitor . . . / with suit and beard and Malacca cane,* which came to one the night in the caffeine night of sleep, reluctantly, put together as *You, island in this page,* read the story of your beginning, how you *watch yourself pass* into the sound words project holding a place in air. The story is simple, an affair to so speak of *Sun,* meaning here *the pages spread out/ before you in the sun,* of mirrors lining *a word beside itself* with parts of the body one at length recalls. At times *a tone of light/ . . . behind the eye,* at times mnemonic, *House: herself in the mirror photographing herself.* There is space to be filled with *bodies, a now here and a now gone* sense of what the voices would say to us had we heard them stripped to essential *zero code/ system of assemblage and separation* knowing the world as *Mica, Money, 'dust and moths.'* Reports from the edge of the region have been mixed, *'mute as stalks'// ('moths')* that flicker out when the light goes *where we've come to sleep;* the implication of acts we thought of as language made self-evident now becomes *the Côte des Morts she writes,* the *counterlight// in the fluid window;* an engine in the street fired on, *narrowed, searching for a lost head;* an horizon the next morning in whose thought clarity as near as wind *is a word, for example, meaning violence.*

Sun here means *words elsewhere. Objects elsewhere and the words to revive them* as one leans back against the quilt against the wall, made up in the actual image of hours with*in the radius of a phrase* memory holds as its own, an image as it were imprinted on the page folded precisely open to *the problem we began with, that words have no letters* to mark the self they would announce, the engine in the chest whose pistons drive a little, a little more. *Come and look* the guide says of the *Sun,* meaning here *'Now you cannot speak/ and now . . .'* you will. *Because there is a literal shore* you hear the sea at the end of the street, waves on the seawall when the tide is high and the swell from the west, or northwest, *or the source of each color/ at a table by a wall.* Painted finish, maybe copper, marble, gold leaf *thread to thread/ there are pieces of the* voices of others scattered along the margin the water washes back.

A geometry of point, counterpoint, the phone rings to open act 3, scene 1, *this instance of playing* out of date, a poem in which *You are the negative*—urge, impulse, a man on his knees nailing shingles. There is a time for it the circle will close *there on the screen,* say, *say a particular music* the book as written plays the morning you sit in the window, listening to it. The feeling is of *no ink/ there you were not a photograph* but the person in it, a half smile maybe, *ordinary, the same/ as language only smaller. It's called* a ship traveling the line of horizon, *no picture at all* in the sense by which I mean a person across the street who cries out *No then yes* turns to her child, who is grown now, *then divides.* Just at that moment the whole of their life together *travels through her teeth,* coughs, scratches an arm the sun has begun to color, *Sun* meaning here again *asymptote, locus, tear or tear* the words from the page, pages from the spine of the book. An approach to who possesses then the phrase itself meant by book, a life contemplative, as in *this paper I'm holding,* notes one thinks to make in lieu of coffee together, say in *the shining windows* this morning, yesterday *the well, the needle's eye.*

The ceiling measures as tall as the tree *Those pyramids yet to come* will house, overhead *something else I wanted to say* in the sentence only just forgot (*its question to the poem* a matter less of continuous *fragments of a face* you look after as it turns, resolving itself, than the position you take vis-à-vis the unnamed edge between blue of sky and blue of water), *a place from which you watch* the words whose aim recalls *the person I miss, the down on her lip.* Disembodied almost, half dressed and half not, *Sun* on her arm meaning high pressure, clear for days, *it could be said that we floated.*

And so like parts of the body, *neither eyes nor ears,* I find myself in thought *a word beside itself* grown to meaning *paint on the walls* the lines themselves border, this story, this assumed approach. On the one hand remember steps up the stair, *To the left of the piano is theory* made concrete, *call it Trace/ B says* shrugging his shoulders, turning down the street. A suggestion of music at this point, off stage left, meaning *This is sleep/ who meets you there* beside the cat, who decides to sleep a moment in the sun. *Sun* meaning here the *neck and hip to bend just so,* another view as the *word twists backward* over itself, into the air, ear, *shadow or shape hidden by sound.*

Passages in italics are from *Sun* (Berkeley: North Point Press, 1988).

Supernatural Duet

> When the Troubadour poets, when the Chinese poets and Japanese poets collaborated, certainly it was a collaboration in that each person put forth in his or her part of the collaboration their best effort—their absolute best effort. And the person following that effort would equally want to put forth their best effort.
>
> —Ted Berrigan, *Talking in Tranquility*

Ted Berrigan thought of collaboration in writing as a form of competition—not so much as in sports say, an aging George Foreman going the distance with Evander Holyfield, who gets the unanimous decision (barely), but rather as "two boys with a ball, and one saying, 'See if you can do this trick.' And then doing a trick. And then the other one doing it, and then it's his turn to say, 'See if you can do this one.'" The essence of the art is play: "Play as a synonym for competition. Competition as a synonym for play. And the dominant feeling that comes out of that is joy. Joy and pleasure. What one gets literally off of watching beautifully skilled teams of acrobats."[1]

If the players on this "team" are two poets, each engaged in a game devised according to whatever rules they decide upon, the poem that results will be neither one nor the other's but a *shared* work, the page it occupies a *shared* space: their words in effect *co-operative,* the result of labor expended together—"labor" going back to the Latin sense of to glide or slip, hence to fail, leading by extension to the noun sense of weight, under which one staggers. To collaborate, then, divides the labor needed to produce a work between two persons, each of whom shares the burden of that weight, assumes responsibility for delivering a part of the product, in this case to the page upon whose blankness words arrive from a *pair* of minds, two voices rather than one. A form of singing together say, the soprano and alto if that's the range (or alto and tenor or tenor and bass), the one leading the other or vice versa, or both going together at the same time, synchronically. A form that's "not private" (Berrigan), competitive in that each partner gives it his or her all, "in order to get the intensity, the intense seriousness, of the feeling that one is trying to have come forth and be present in whatever one is writing."[2] What results is in a sense hybrid, greater (at least other) than the sum of its two parts.

That "sum" in the case of Ron Padgett and Clark Coolidge's *Supernatural Overtones* (Great Barrington, MA: The Figures, 1990) presents a framework through which to see (visualize) a representation of the *co-operation-of-words-in-poem-as-words-on-page.* To begin with, the page here is conceived of as a "square," a flat box so to speak of its two dimensions (7″ × 8 ½″, thus to the eye nearly square) upon which are placed four lines in what looks to be the shape of a square (actually it's a 6″ × 5″ rectangle) floating "off center" an inch from the top of the page, 2 ½″ from the bottom, so that the immediate effect of the whole page creates a sense of *askewness*—a shape in (and of) lines that suggests but is not a square, set not squarely on a page that itself suggests but is not a square.

Add to that set-up (all but blank) words: a few words only printed inside the "box" (Coolidge's contribution, though never identified as such) below which is printed (in a different typeface) a sentence or two (Padgett's), as in this example from the first (unnumbered) page:

been some
them there
that these
things

A green and jagged stone hand comes to life.

Or take this even more minimal (more insistently less intrusive) instance from page 4:

to and felt

An invisible employee decides to impersonate the company president.

One locates these poems in the region Coolidge explored in *Space* (1970), whose word placements in the space of the white page did things to that page—and to our sense of what might transpire there—that his words in this book do as well:

back then

been while

An archeological expedition discovers the mummy of Im-Ho-Tep in an Egyptian tomb. Years later, Im-Ho-Tep, who has come to life, directs another expedition, this one to the tomb of an Egyptian princess.

—as if time then (and so space) *could* be registered as or in a form of words. Taking place below the "square" (that is not square) box, Padgett's contributions to *Supernatural Overtones* might be seen as "captions" to Coolidge's word "pictures"—which stand then not as an image but object, one that invites us to "see" in language as a medium (object/thing) the materiality of the text, the book itself as a physics ideas live in, in words. Or perhaps Padgett's sentences are the ground bass below or upon which Coolidge's higher (voice) register plays its complementary music. Thus below the box enclosing "back then / been while" one reads what could be an account, or other "notes," or other language (even though it's still English), as if any two speakers' "take" on anything might never quite coincide: "An archeological expedition discovers the mummy of Im-Ho-Tep in an Egyptian tomb. Years later, Im-Ho-Tep, who has come to life, directs another expedition, this one to the tomb of an Egyptian princess." Circularity as a form of thinking (the form of dreams) may be embodied both spatially (as in Coolidge) and in narrative (Padgett), a form traditionally based on the concept of time as a line, traveling "forward" (past—present—future), the line prone to twist, bend, break, or otherwise interrupt its "progress," the train that jumps its tracks:

id
murray accident
  march hum eft cheese
board glad ask
ark plaid mouse
        please lain

cart latin
sleet sift bulbous
nun cat
race mast pinch
bum
     alum latin

When a friend is injured in a battle with gangsters, a brain specialist gives him the brain of a dying gangster, in a dream. All three wake up in Honolulu.

To put it differently, the surprise one finds in dreams lies in the extraordinary juxtaposition of what *by themselves* would be the most ordinary of details: "When twenty-year old Kay Banks announces she's going to get married, the entire Banks household is thrown into a canyon." Surprise of a similar kind takes place here in the superimposition of (two writers') tones. Words which by themselves are ordinary—*gong, knot, whelm, niece, dice, pars*—when placed in spatial configuration with each other *as the poem* (in the box, thus framed, so a word picture) take on a supernatural capacity to move into, or act as conduit from, some realm of thought/speech we don't normally have access to:

gong
knot whelm
niece
dice
pars

In Japan crickets are kept in cages and used as watchdogs. If a stranger approaches during the night, the crickets stop chirping and start barking.

Couple to this "knot" of words—the overtone? if so, above which (narrative) bass its note resonates—the result of Padgett's co-labor, whose role one might take as "text" to Coolidge's (visual) "cartoon"—the fiction say, or documentary report, or even one thinks translation from what amounts to some edge or periphery of English, a border region say whose laws of syntax and reference seem not yet to have been set down—an only seemingly straightforward sentence, "correct" enough grammatically however weird its spokes and spin: "In Japan crickets are kept in cages and used as watchdogs. If a stranger approaches during the night, the crickets stop chirping and start barking."

In writing this "bicycle" built for two, neither Padgett nor Coolidge could have written *Supernatural Overtones* by himself. Each needed the cooperation of the other—the one who did what he did best best—and each gave to the other what otherwise wasn't given, and so couldn't be found. Singing together, *not writing alone,* their work here above all an investigation of the act(s) by which language makes of the world a fiction, and of that fiction a world:

thing
same
can
are

A bull terrier rises from Bowery to blue ribbons.

Knowledge

The passages opposed to one another stand on the same white page. At each reading the voice intones certain words, gasps, continues. He was breathing and the blood "welled out of him" like knowledge, the moth in the windowsill "relaxed, and instantly grew stiff."

One's sentences stop at the place where the next action takes over. A pencil, rifle, human beings in the city, at work in fields. The feeling of what is called the event is always different.

In another world people will be useless, "powerless to move," nobody to know the effort required to tell (again) or read (again) the account of each creature's moment of equality.

Whoever wants to read this account may also choose to be moved by it, as in writing the pencil equals itself (again). This seems to make no impression. The next moment the legs "continued" the throat.

Nevertheless, when the body is cold one sees "the far-off smoke of houses," faces behind the knowledge that the window is closed. To write of this thought consider its failure: something that "must" make the story strange as friction.

The shape of energy relaxes into the shape of words. During his whole life, the man realized an enormous exhaustion was about to begin. This is one way of thinking like a machine.

Properly speaking, the knowledge of writing is endless. By this I do not mean "anything" in particular, how someone could be displayed at the end of circumspection, a wider circle "thrown into the air."

After the spectacle he did what he could to avoid looking (when the mouth is open it is perfectly clear). To say this on the third or fourth day after one knows it had stopped, time stood still. One is apt to keep thinking beyond the personal.

To be conscious from ear to ear, consider the damage of "shot after shot" pouring into the body. In the end I am thinking of an imaginary animal significant only in that it moves me onward to other matters.

Afterwards, the "desperate slowness" of light as it settled on the window submerged any thought of what had happened. One is left, possibly for the first time, with corners in the margin to indicate where the next thought has collapsed.

The only time it reappeared *in terror,* the wrong direction in place of knowledge as something about to happen. Suddenly the experience seems "the width of the sky," not a chance to thrust the body into its shape, momentarily hollow.

I perceived the road over my shoulder, people at the bottom of a trench. I made up my mind that the people were a story, no more dangerous than a moth asleep at the edge of the window. It was impossible not to feel the agony of the corpses pressing forward.

Opinion divided in the middle of a pause, thinking the brain was on the side against which it struggled. It was different now that thought could be realized, now that I think of it. Besides the condition wanted to eat.

The figure who remained a second in the corner, thinking from side to side of the body across a field of words, friction, impossibly perfect hills. Someone content with what appears to be his fate, settled in a shadow of minutes where the window had been.

The possibilities of pleasure a third time, rising and falling to the ground in front of another shape to be noticed, wanted (it seems) in thinking of moisture beyond the air, the number of voices in a distance enough to be seen.

It is useless to be born in another shape, as if what happened on the ground seemed to collapse in spite of feeling moved. Then, suddenly, the thought arrived in front of the mouth, continued breathing.

To perceive at that distance the certainty of their opinion, the antagonist who will protest the "romantic voice," circumspection being limited to looking at the circle as "something marvellous" in the shape of the world.

Whether the others missed a step or sound merely of waiting, "native" important enough to see what apparently happened in the possibilities of a different approach to thinking (another man) or waiting (that look).

Consider his attempt to be nothing visible, thought divided between the "diminutive" body and its *large* leg, a pause if you missed it in the sense that the mind is irresistibly "hollow" the moment he destroys it.

In one direction, the crowd "must" be possible. One could not forget to relax, but in "reality" the condition of the body "twisted to one side" seems to lead to an effort against what it means to know.

The shadow of a particular morning, a different person at the corner "a hundred yards away" from the scene in a story the experience of which is comparable to being stopped.

The tongue was going to be shot, "going to be shot" an expression the eye caught looking up into the air or waiting to start again at the bottom of the book "as one waits for a machine."

A perspective in the previous person turned over, questions tolerable at a distance feeling the politics of knowledge, light pressing forward without thinking of his leg, figure, or the faces behind it.

The mind of the woman composed at the end, the third or fourth shape beyond the square, information continued as if "into the same spot" reduced to being sideways or forward instead of straight.

Again to know "what had happened," conscious of the part it appeared to play in wanting to move back or pause (always) at the edge of that impression, "he seemed to say" the sentence had been chosen.

Axis of Simultaneities

> After being perceived several times, objects acquire the status of "recognition." An object appears before us. We know it's there but we do not see it, and, for that reason we can say nothing about it. The removal of this object from the sphere of automatized perception is accomplished in art by a variety of devices.
>
> —Victor Shklovsky, *Theory of Prose*

In order to say something about the "object," how can writing make us "see" it as it is in fact, as if for the first time? One thinks, for instance, of a writing that could give us perceptions and thoughts in (and about) the experience of reading itself, whereby the apprehension of a text becomes analogous to apprehension of the world. The "story" as we know it will be informed by itself, by the twists and turns and edges of a language that calls attention as much to the seams in the artifice as to the narrative it pretends to disclose.

The Novel / A Poem by Paul Hoover (New York: New Directions, 1990) investigates the ways in which such a writing might break apart the structures of information by which art tries to hold its mirror up to nature. In place of representation, it puts forward a "view" of the world that is fully conscious of the part it plays as words in a performance of the world one knows through language—"The world was meaningful—/no sentence could alter that"—the implication of whose structures leads us through reading to the creation of meanings that contain, but are not contained by, those structures. Like sound bytes pieced together without "transition," *The Novel* echoes the voices whose tradition it is heir to—Western literature, American culture, literary criticism, journalism, advertising, popular songs—"Life is/ filled with bitter tears, on a/ highway called the Blues." Its fragments refuse to give us the comfort of a constructed whole into whose surface (sensuous details, the landscape of fiction as window through which one sees an illusion of people in the world) the reader may be absorbed. These interruptions, it turns out, work as the "device" by which "automatized perception" (in narrative as in life) is short-circuited, making way for the perception of elements as and for what they are.

In reading *The Novel,* one keeps getting tripped up, keeps having to adjust his or her sense of what is going on as the work, which keeps shifting, unfolds itself. With each change of the lens—now this "story" now that—the illusion of reality in a narrative-as-window-on-the-world gets shattered—

> The hero shrank
> into past tense, becoming a lexical vapor

> between the wind and thee.
> Half an hour later, he was nothing more
> than an inward bruise, smudge
> of something read.
> Foot, feet; tooth, teeth; goose, geese.
> Travel, ravel, trave.
> Ouilimette, Illinois. Written out of life.

The Novel (art) isn't as Aristotle claimed an imitation, it's as real as (thinking) reality itself. The collage of its fragments is central to the project its words project in their mapping of the space "She was by, of, about and at./ The sentence performed a phonic act." Reading it, we aren't able to lull ourselves into the fabric of a novel (or poem) as narrative. Rather, the disjunction of each leap displaces us into yet another frame (of reference) or tone (of voice), one heard or viewed as if from a different angle—"It was almost a song, nearly a speech after dinner,/ alas on loan, amassed a fortune, amo, amas, amat."

One reads *The Novel* not for its "story" but in order to read, and thereby to know, the world as words whose interplay make it (world) fully present. Instead of assuming the reader's response to fiction as representation, its writing is conscious of and pleased by its capacity to make illusion—"The white body of words isn't a woman or man./ It's the shape that carries them both,/ shaking like meat, insolvent as water." As much about itself and the process of its composition as it is about Paul Hoover's sense of the world—"the novelist rose like blue liquid/ through the 'surface realism'/ of each invented self, existing only/ when quietly going out of existence,/ vaguely seen by the measured eye"—it does not forget (and in effect pays homage to) its own devices—

> The "scaffold of self"
> was being built in a bedroom
> She climbed into a climate of ego and desire.
> But what would Serena do, now that she was a name?

As a result, our perceptions take place in the real time of reading—present tense, always immediate—thereby avoiding simple "recognition," which Stein understood to be the generalizing function of memory ("Remembering is repetition . . . the repetition consists in knowing that that one is a kind of a one"), a habitual response to particular phenomena that is always at least one step removed from moment-by-moment perception of the thing itself. Instead of linear plot, *The Novel / A Poem* gives us the possibility that narrative might go forward by turning in upon itself in concentric circles, like Chinese boxes within boxes, its framework discovered each (new) sentence by sentence. "Because Art/ is the act of dissimulation. Making still/ is making strange. Metaphor freezes and changes./ Thought is refractory. Narrative follows/ a curving line," the poem-as-novel/ novel-as-poem unfolds layers of itself as itself—"He [the novelist] was about to enter the building/ where he himself sat in a chair,/ reading the novel in which this happens." Interruption—of sequence of events, of voices in a narrative structure that never quite materializes but remains instead marginal—traces the ineffable body of a story that keeps striving to be "told" (and keeps failing)—

> Mandy stepped through the door.
> She was beautiful and wise.
> He placed his lips in the cleft
> of her neck and heard the soothing words.
> In his hand was the novel
> in which she lived and breathed.

When writing echoes voices clearly other than the writer's own, one gets the sense of writer as ventriloquist, or actor capable of taking many parts (none of them "his," all of them "his"), the poem not so much an expression of self as construct of devices whose sound/image enacts the mind/sense at work. So through Hoover one "rehears" Shakespeare—"I will be brief. Your noble son is mad"—Herbert—"Decaying more and more,/ 'til he became Most poore"—Sterne—"'A white bear! Very well. Have I ever seen one?/ Might I ever have seen one. Am I ever to see one?'"—Williams—"So much depends/ upon/ a red morpheme/ glazed with commas/ beside the white/ inflexion"—and even Hoover's own novel—"In Saigon, Illinois/ night shifts on the home front/ a television war"—each instance followed by non-sequitur whose sense doesn't "fit" the context, and so realizes the indeterminacy of our condition. Observation—knowledge—depends upon the position or angle of the observer—"as soon as 'I' adopt it/ the mode is already gone."

The Novel / A Poem takes place along what Hoover calls "An axis of simultaneities,/ where . . . evil leaps but never lands"—"evil" in this case being each instance of language, image, idea, voice or "thread" taken up momentarily, only to be interrupted, dropped or lost. The language of popular culture is fractured by the language of literary form—"Please leave your name/ at the sound of the sonnet"—literary criticism by the language of golf—"In a style that is supple, spare,/ and unsentimental. Bliss, passion,/ and great one-liners. Finding a driver/ that matches your swing; making friends/ with the long irons." Because, as *The Novel* tells us, "fiction/ practices fragmentation, then/ we enter the ruined museum," echoes of a cast of voices are broken into by yet more echoes—"Geneologies, chronicles, duplicates,/ notes, lists, tales, accounts/ copies, citations, archives, inventories,/ monuments, reproductions, simulacra, fakes." As "If mankind dreamt collectively," Hoover's "ruined museum" is nothing less than our location in American culture, circa 1990, a collection of fragments that *The Novel*—a profoundly political poem—shores up against our ruin.

The Landscape (Body) of the Poem

To speak of the poem as a landscape—the body of the world—will be to think of the geography of its features: peninsulas, rivers, valleys, mountains, oceans; fingers, arms, legs, bones, brain.

The image represents a form of the world it knows in (of) words and elements (letters/spaces) within and between words, which are themselves as essential as words.

Where words come from, where they go: that is to say, how words come out of the body and re-enter it; how the world of the body "spells" the word and is, reciprocally, "spelled" by it; how we know what we know of what we know.

Words a *form* of the body, like skin: "I rub my language against the other," Barthes writes, "as if I had words instead of fingers, or fingers at the tip of my words."

Words read by the eye, heard by the ear, measure the person whose thought they become, what is going on in that body (physical) registered as that series of sounds—and silences between sounds, acoustic motion and stops—that record the moment of composition of "world event" as well as (only) a person's thought in words.

When the poem is read aloud it enters the air as a timed, literally linear ("one after another") sounding of language perceived not by the eye but ear, not as words seen but sounds (and silence) heard.

To read a poem that asks a reader what it means to read a poem, that questions the experience of reading words that question that experience: what is the sound of "bird singing"?

The sound of words in the air is the sound of thought and thought of sound; the sound of knowledge in articulate present the moment words come up off the page; the sound of the world as it is shaped in words.

Its music is what it thinks to say in the rhythm (of lines) and pitch (of syllables or silence) whose "voice" is literally an ("echo") articulation of sound.

The poem as "echo" remembers words that others speak and write—the past becoming present at each instant of that writing, rehearsing (re : hear : sing) what one doesn't know until then.

The text positions itself on the page, a function of a surface (contour) whose rhythm *also* (somehow) "magically" records the shape of thought, feeling, and/or perception (knowledge).

The mapping begins with a pencil. What is not known can be said to be said. What is known cannot be said.

Sometimes one has the feeling that the next word will be [white], a blank that stands in place of what is missing, either not yet formed or eroded away.

Words contiguous to one another, their proximity making itself felt in the room that is air, will take possession of the eye reading, ear listening to the sound they make themselves by.

One will read the poem as one touches a body that is not yet (or no longer) familiar: the moment of each word inviting an "adjustment"—of the hand or reception of thought—to what is being at that moment written (felt).

A wind shifting from south to northwest means the front has passed. So does the preceding sentence, whose means are words—a kind of weather.

Somewhere else the same poem is written by someone else: the person who reads it, the person who enacts the "same" text (next).

Language equals charge, the poem's language charge squared (or to the nth degree)—"at the round earth's imagin'd corners, blow": writing both an acoustic and, on the page, spatial index of thought, "weather" in language itself.

What takes place on the page is in that sense a physical analogue to what the ear hears when the poem is read, the act of listening being an extension of the act of writing.

To say *the poem is* (literally) *the body* suggests its relation to the person who writes it: the finger-tip as much as -print, the body itself a measure (instance) of its life, the light (around it) more than the shadow (it casts).

That is to say, the poem is an extension of the writer's/reader's body and its own body, coming out of one and being one, its letters (spaces) in a language whose shape on the page and in the air spells what it means to write/read.

(Reading) the poem is *rereading,* simply in the sense that its words (language) precede it. The poem is built of *remembered* (used) *materials* the poet finds somewhere in a world (of words) that has been seen or heard before.

The time of the poem, the time of the body in the world: as landscape changes depending on the time of day or year, weather conditions, the position of the observer, the poem is also "changed" ("charged") at each (re)reading.

"And what should I do in Illyria,/ My brother he is in Elysium," Viola says in *Twelfth Night,* sending out a current of multiple sparks that jumps across the synapse between "Illyria" and "Elysium," *through* the ear by way of (words) the syllable.

Words of a complexity vaster than we comprehend—"monuments" like buildings in a landscape whose rooms, windows, doors and halls we walk through, wondering, "What did they do here?" "How did they live?"

How in Orsino's words at the beginning of *Twelfth Night,* "If music be the food of love, play on,/ Give me excess of it, that, surfeiting,/ The appetite may sicken, and so die," language goes forward from world to world: the angle of a mind landing on its feet, lifting off again, bearing meaning out the door.

How this statement seems to make perfect "sense" to the reader—until the net of syntax springs the animal meaning would be, releasing what I think I know.

Think of the weight echo bears as it moves from one person's set of words—which themselves have had a "prior life" in these or other frames of coherence.

How what is made "new" at any time in the life of language stands on the shoulders of the one before the one before, "stout Cortez . . . Silent, upon a peak in Darien" peering onward, forward, for the (next) words.

Writing a kind of "memory": to cast a net across the whole field of possible words, draw together those that maximize as much of what has been "said" before, and will be "said" from now on: how else to know perception, my present feeling, thought's pulse.

Words that think and feel the world, perceive what the person finds as continually present as past, the poem is always "landscape": as painting is always pigment, drawing the line, music a sequence of pitches played in time.

Think of the line whose unfurling of words blows from where one hasn't yet been, whose "progress" word-to-word or turn at the line break startles: after leaving its moment of silence on the white page, what starts over becomes next in a series of sounds whose time/line has come.

Say that words have a life of their own; that the line is infinite as far as we know; that clouds float in its blue to the southeast; that it may or may not "form" to the left, the full moon "fall" on the fifteenth.

The thought of the voice falling on the penultimate note, syllable, sound, takes hold of the ear in the space between gestures, the silences before and after the line that floats in the white of eye's page, tongue's tooth, in such terms.

Such words appear on the page as a form of movement, having landed there (or been placed) as if arriving from the air or (other) page the poet thought to breathe (read breath).

Erosion of land by the action of water and wind: the poem also a new form of the world (reincarnation) that is writing itself. What is called writing (as well as "literature") becomes in fact a geology of the body of all possible words.

What *is* written *has been* written, in other words.

What is new in writing is what one (it) doesn't know. The saw cuts the branch meaning there is another shape to the tree, which has been displaced (or placed *elsewhere*) in a position that is no longer the (same) tree.

Somewhere else the body appears in the same words (landscape) as before, where it will be different, the poem that becomes itself as one who listens will know, assuming the presence of that person whose life is the narrative the poem means to record.

Narrative, no matter what shape it comes in, may be understood as the terms whose order in the poem shapes it on the page and in the air, as fragments of a life (transcribed) made present in the act of writing.

These pieces—letters in words, words in the line, gaps between them, marks of punctuation, breaks—mean to be seen by the eye, heard by the ear, as analogue (approximate) to the "I" who is writing itself; that person therefore here as "echo," as the poem by which "I" writes.

The poem is everything (and everything that is missing) its words say: what is missing means to be known as another form of (prior) knowledge, private in the sense that one knows "internal difference/ Where the Meanings, are—"

Listening to the poem "When it comes, the Landscape listens" to hear itself (again) in the words that resound its body.

Notes

. . . sound . . . shape . . . meaning . . .

1. See especially, however, these notable exceptions: Bruce Andrews, *Paradise & Method: Poetics & Praxis* (Evanston, IL: Northwestern University Press, 1996); Charles Bernstein, *Content's Dream: Essays 1975–1984* (Los Angeles: Sun & Moon Press, 1986) and *A Poetics* (Cambridge, MA: Harvard University Press, 1992); Don Byrd, *The Poetics of the Common Knowledge* (Albany: SUNY Press, 1994); John Cage, *Musicage: Cage Muses on Word Art Music,* ed. Joan Retallack (Hanover, NH: Wesleyan University Press, 1996); Michael Davidson, *Ghostlier Demarcations: Modern Poetry and the Material Word* (Berkeley and Los Angeles: University of California Press, 1997); Alan Davies, *Signage* (New York: Roof Books, 1987); Johanna Drucker, *Figuring the Word: Essays on Writing, Books, and Visual Poetics* (New York: Granary Books, 1998); Rachel Blau DuPlessis, *The Pink Guitar: Writing as Feminist Practice* (New York: Routledge, 1990); Larry Eigner, *areas lights heights: Writings 1954–1989* (New York: Roof Books, 1989); George Hartley, *Textual Politics and the Language Poets* (Bloomington: Indiana University Press, 1989); Dick Higgens, *Horizons* (Carbondale: Southern Illinois University Press, 1982); Nathaniel Mackey, *Discrepant Engagement: Dissonace, Cross-Culturality, and Experimental Writing* (Cambridge and New York: Cambridge University Press, 1993); Steve McCaffery, *North of Intention: Critical Writings, 1973–1980* (New York: Roof Books, 1986); Bob Perelman, *The Trouble with Genius: Reading Pound, Joyce, Stein, and Zukofsky* (Berkeley and Los Angeles: University of California Press, 1994) and *The Marginalization of Poetry* (Evanston, IL: Northwestern Univeristy Press, 1996); Marjorie Perloff, *The Futurist Moment: Avant-Garde, Avant Guerre, and the Language of Rupture* (Chicago: University of Chicago Press, 1986), *The Poetics of Indeterminancy: Rimbaud to Cage* (Evanston, IL: Northwestern University Press, 1983), *Radical Artifice: Writing Poetry in the Age of Media* (Chicago: University of Chicago Press, 1991), and *Wittgenstein's Ladder* (Chicago: University of Chicago Press, 1996); Peter Quartermain, *Disjunctive Poetics* (Cambridge and New York: Cambridge University Press, 1992); Linda Reinfeld, *Language Poetry: Writing as Rescue* (Baton Rouge: Louisiana State University Press, 1992); Leslie Scalapino, *How Phenomena Appear To Unfold* (Elmwood, CT: Potes & Poets Press, 1990) and *The Public World/Syntactically Impermanence* (Hanover, VT and London: Wesleyan University Press, 1999); Ron Silliman, *The New Sentence* (New York: Roof Books, 1987); Robert von Hallberg, *Politics & Poetic Value* (Chicago: University of Chicago Press, 1987); Barrett Watten, *Total Syntax* (Carbondale: Southern Illinois University Press, 1985).

See also the following anthologies of recent critical writings: Bruce Andrews and Charles Bernstein, eds., *The L=A=N=G=U=A=G=E Book* (Carbondale: Southern Illinois University Press, 1984); Charles Bernstein, ed., *The Politics of Poetic Form: Poetry* *and Public Policy* (New York: Roof Books, 1990); Manuel Brito, ed., *A Suite of Poetic Voices: Interviews with Contemporary American Poets* (Santa Brigida, Portugal: Kadle Books, 1992); Philip Foss and Charles Bernstein, eds., *Patterns / Contexts / Time: A Symposium on Contemporary Poetry* (Santa Fe: Tyuonyi, 1990); Peter Gizzi, ed., "Writing from the New Coast: Presentation," *o*blek* 12 (Stockbridge, MA: The Garlic Press, 1993); Michael Palmer, ed., *Code of Signals* (Berkeley: North Atlantic Books, 1983); Bob Perelman, ed., *Talks* (San Francisco: Hills, 1980) and *Writing/Talks* (Carbondale: Southern Illinois University Press, 1985); Marjorie Perloff and Charles Junkerman, eds., *John Cage: Composed in America* (Chicago: University of Chicago Press, 1994); Ron Silliman, ed., *In the American Tree: Language, Poetry, Realism* (Orono, ME: The National Poetry Foundation, 1986); Mary Margaret Sloan, ed., *Moving Borders: Three Decades of Innovative Writing by Women* (Jersey City: Talisman House, 1998); Juliana Spahr et al., eds., *A Poetics of Criticism* (Buffalo, NY: LEAVE books, 1994) and *Writing from the New Coast* (Buffalo, NY: LEAVE books, 1994); Anne Waldman and Andrew Schelling, eds., *Disembodied Poetics: Annals of the Jack Kerouac School* (Albuquerque: University of New Mexico Press, 1994).

2. John Cage, "Forward," *Silence* (Middletown, CT: Wesleyan University Press, 1983), ix.

3. Julia Kristeva, writing on "the word within the space of texts," posits a related but different conception of the three-dimensionality of the poetic text: "To investigate the status of the word is to study its articulations (as semic complex) with other words in the sentence, and then to look for the same functions or relationships at the articulatory level of larger sequences. Confronted with this spatial conception of language's poetic operation, we must first define the three dimensions of textual space where various semic sets and poetic sequences function. These three dimensions or coordinates of dialogue are writing subject, addressee and exterior texts. The word's status is thus defined *horizontally* (the word in the text belongs to both writing subject and addressee) as well as *vertically* (the word in the text is oriented towards an anterior or synchronic literary corpus)." "Word, Dialogue and Novel," *The Kristeva Reader*, ed. Toril Moi (New York: Columbia University Press, 1986), 36–37. Compare Barthes's model of a different three-dimensionality: "A language is therefore a horizon, and style a vertical dimension, which together map out for the writer a Nature." "*Writing Degree Zero*," trans. Annette Lavers and Colin Smith (New York: Farrar, Straus and Giroux, 1968), 13.

4. Charles Olson, "Projective Verse," *Selected Writings* (New York: New Directions, 1966), 16.

5. See for example Helen Vendler on Stevens's echoes of Keats: "The end of 'Sunday Morning' is a rewritten version of the close of Keats's 'To Autumn.' . . . However, Stevens as a modern poet, offers no single doctrine but rather a choice among truths: we live either (1) in chaos, or (2) in a system of mutual dependency, or (3) in a condition of solitude, which may itself be seen as (3a) lonely ('unsponsored') or (3b) liberated ('free'), but which is an any case inescapable. The passage allowing doctrinal choices is followed by the passage on deer, quail, berries, and pigeons (those wilderness forms replacing Keats's domestic ones), in which the doctrinal options are alluded to but, in the end, left undecided. . . . In the end, as the pigeons inscribe their

transient motions in the air, their calligraphy is read (by the poet seeking significance) as elusively ambiguous, and doctrinal choice dissolves in mystery. But although metaphysical certainty remains unattainable, the truth of existence is clear. The final motion, whether or not definable as one of chaos, dependency, solitude, freedom or unsponsoredness, is 'downward to darkness.' In such an ending, *be* is the finale of *seem,* and death is the only certainty uninvaded by metaphysical doubt. While Keats rests in the polyphony of the creatures in their autumnal choir, Stevens (though his adoption of Keats's principal trope, enumeration, shows him as not insensible to the plentitude around him in the scene) makes his landscape depend for its significance on what it can explicitly suggest about metaphysical truth" (*Part of Nature, Part of Us: Modern American Poets* [Cambridge, MA: Harvard University Press, 1980] 22–23).

6. Charles Bernstein, "Artifice of Absorption," *A Poetics* (Cambridge, MA: Harvard University Press, 1992), 10 (my italics).

7. Ludwig Wittgenstein, *Zettel* (Berkeley and Los Angeles: University of California Press, 1970), 33e.

8. Theodor Adorno, *Aesthetic Theory* (London: Routledge & Kegan Paul, 1984), 6.

9. Lev Vygotsky, "Thought and Word," *Thought and Language* (Cambridge: MIT Press, 1986), 212. See also the following, "Thought is born through words"; "Experience teaches us that thought does not express itself in words, but rather realizes itself in them" (255, 251).

10. Gertrude Stein, "Matisse," *A Stein Reader,* ed. Ulla Dydo (Evanston, IL: Northwestern University Press, 1993), 141.

11. Stein, "Sentences and Paragraphs," *How to Write* (New York: Dover Publications, 1975), 29.

12. Stein, *The Making of Americans: Being a History of a Family's Progress, A Stein Reader,* 55.

13. Louis Zukofsky, "An Objective," *Prepositions: The Collected Critical Essays of Louis Zukofsky* (Berkeley and Los Angeles: University of California Press, 1981), 12.

14. Ibid., 17.

15. Stein, "Two Women," *A Stein Reader,* 113.

16. Vygotsky, *Thought and Language,* 222.

17. Martin Heidegger, "The Anaximander Fragment," *Early Greek Thinking,* trans. David Farrell Krell and Frank A. Capuzzi (San Francisco: Harper & Row, 1984), 54.

Con( )Text

1. Ludwig Wittgenstein, *Zettel* (Berkeley and Los Angeles: University of California Press, 1970), 28e.

2. Alan Davies, "Language/ Mind/ Writing," *Signage* (New York: Roof Books, 1987), 121.

3. Robert Grenier, "On Speech," *In The American Tree: Language, Poetry, Realism* ed. Ron Silliman, (Orono, ME: The National Poetry Foundation, 1986), 496.

4. Charles Bernstein, "Stray Straws and Straw Men," *Content's Dream: Essays 1975–1984* (Los Angeles: Sun & Moon Press, 1986), 45.

5. Ron Silliman, "LANGUAGE, REALISM, POETRY," *In the American Tree,* xvi.

6. Bernstein, "Thought's Measure," *Content's Dream,* 61–62.

7. Wittgenstein, *Zettel,* 12e.

8. Grenier, "On Speech," 497.

9. Gertrude Stein, "Portraits and Repetition," *Writing and Lectures 1909–1945,* ed. Patricia Meyerowitz (Baltimore: Penguin Books, 1971), 115.

10. Tina Darragh, "Procedure," *The L=A=N=G=U=A=G=E Book* (Carbondale: Southern Illinois University Press, 1984), 108.

11. Rosmarie Waldrop, "Alarms & Excursions," *The Politics of Poetic Form: Poetry and Public Policy,* ed. Charles Bernstein (New York: Roof Books, 1990), 54.

12. Jackson Mac Low, "'Language-Centered,'" *In the American Tree,* 492.

13. Louis Zukofsky, "An Objective," *Prepositions: The Collected Critical Essays of Louis Zukofsky* (Berkeley and Los Angeles: University of California Press, 1981), 14.

14. Clark Coolidge, "From a Letter to Paul Metcalf (jan 7 1972)," *In The American Tree,* 501.

15. Grenier, "Hedge-crickets Sing," *The L=A=N=G=U=A=G=E Book,* 20.

16. Zukofsky, "An Objective," 17.

17. Wittgenstein, *Philosophical Investigations* (New York: Macmillan, 1958), 329.

18. Lev Vygotsky, "Thought and Word," *Thought and Language* (Cambridge: MIT Press, 1986), 251.

19. Bernstein, "Thought's Measure," 74.

20. Robert Creeley, *Pieces* (New York: Charles Scribners, 1969), 61.

21. Zukofsky, "A Statement for Poetry," *Prepositions,* 21.

22. Grenier, "Hedge-crickets Sing," 19.

23. Zukofsky, "An Objective," 16.

24. Mac Low, 491.

25. Bernstein, "Semblance," *Content's Dream,* 34.

26. Creeley, "Poems Are a Complex," *The Collected Essays of Robert Creeley* (Berkeley and Los Angeles: University of California Press, 1989), 490.

27. Bruce Andrews, "Text and Context," *The L=A=N=G=U=A=G=E Book,* 35.

28. Wittgenstein, *Zettel,* 57e.

29. Davies, "notes for CONSTRUCTION," *Signage,* 31.

30. Wittgenstein, *Remarks on the Foundations of Mathematics* (Cambridge: MIT Press, 1978), 107.

31. Bernstein, "Thought's Measure," 72.

32. Mac Low, 493.

33. Willem de Kooning, quoted in Clark Coolidge, "From a Letter to Paul Metcalf (jan 7 1972)," 501.

34. Bernstein, "Thought's Measure," 69.

35. Nick Piombino, "Writing and Conceiving," *In the American Tree,* 580.

36. Vygotsky, 256.

37. Bernstein, "Writing and Method," *Content's Dream,* 236.

38. Andrews, "Text & Context," *Paradise & Method: Poetics & Praxis* (Evanston, IL: Northwestern University Press, 1996), 12, 15.

39. Barrett Watten, "Method and *L=A-N=G=U=A=G=E,*" *In the American Tree,* 612.

40. Leslie Scalapino, *The Front Matter, Dead Souls* (Hanover, NH: Wesleyan University Press, 1996), 46.

41. Lyn Hejinian, "for *Change,*" *In the American Tree,* 487.

42. Bernstein, "Stray Straws and Straw Men," 40–41.

43. Waldrop, 53.

44. Watten, 602.

45. Bernstein, "Thought's Measure," 70.

46. Coolidge, "From Notebooks (1976–1982)," *Code of Signals: Recent Writings in Poetics,* ed. Michael Palmer (Berkeley: North Atlantic Books, 1983), 181.

47. Scalapino, "Robert Grenier's 'Scrawl'," *Objects in the Terrifying Tense/ Longing from Taking Place* (New York: Roof Books, 1993), 41.

48. Hejinian, 487.

49. Bernstein, "Thought's Measure," 71.

50. Wittgenstein, *Tractatus Logico-Philosophicus* (London: Routledge, 1992), 27.

The Asymptote of Elsewhere

1. Charles Bernstein, "The Objectives of Meaning: Reading Cavell Reading Wittgenstein," *Content's Dream: Essays 1975–1984* (Los Angeles: Sun & Moon Press, 1986) 167.

2. W. B. Yeats, "The Symbolism of Poetry," *Essays and Introductions* (New York: Macmillan, 1973), 160. Compare the following passages in "Per Amica Silentia Lunae": "we seem at moments to escape from time in what we call prevision, and from place when we see distant things in a dream and in concurrent dreams"; "I seemed to awake from sleep to find my body rigid, and to hear a strange voice speaking these words through my lips as through lips of stone: 'We make an image of him who sleeps, and it is not him who sleeps, and we call it Emmanuel.'" (*W. B. Yeats: Later Essays,* ed. William H. O'Donnell [New York and London: Charles Schribner's Sons, 1994], 26, 32); and in "Swedenborg, Mediums, and the Desolate Places": "there will be voices flitting here and there in darkness, or in the half-light, or it will be the medium himself fallen into trance who will speak, or without a trance write from a knowledge and intelligence not his own" (*Ibid.,* 62).

3. Friedrich Nietzsche, from *Ecce Homo,* quoted in Brewster Ghiselin, *The Creative Process: A Symposium* (Berkeley and Los Angeles: University of California Press, 1952), 209. See also Nietzsche's remarks on the musician ("an oracle, a priest, or more than a priest—a kind of mouthpiece of the absolute, a telephone line of Transcendence. God's ventriloquist. . . .") in *The Geneology of Morals* (Garden City, NY: Doubleday & Company, 1956), 237.

4. Plato, *The Collected Dialogues,* edited by Edith Hamilton (Princeton: Bollingin Foundation/Princeton University Press, 1963), 220.

5. Janet Hobhouse, *Everybody Who Was Anybody* (New York: G. P. Putnam's Sons, 1975), 96.

6. Herbert Marks, "On Prophetic Stammering," *The Yale Journal of Criticism* 1.1 (1987): 4–5.

7. Gertrude Stein, "Tender Buttons," *Writing and Lectures 1909–1945,* ed. Patricia Meyerowitz (Baltimore: Penguin Books, 1971), 195.

8. Marks, 7.

9. Ezra Pound, *ABC of Reading* (New York: New Directions, 1960), 17.

10. Pound, 17–18.

11. Ibid., 18.

12. Glenn Harcourt, "Andreas Vesalius and the Anatomy of Sculpture," *Representations* 17 (1987): 28.

13. Ibid., 33

14. Louis Zukofsky, "Poetry," *Prepositions* (Berkeley and Los Angeles: University of California Press, 1981), 7.

15. Charles Bernstein, "Thought's Measure," *Content's Dream,* 61–62.

16. Zukofsky, 7.

17. Max I. Baym, "Science and Poetry," *Princeton Encyclopedia of Poetry and Poetics* (Princeton: Princeton University Press, 1974), 452.

[Echoes]

1. Virgil Thomson, *Music with Words: A Composer's View* (New Haven and London: Yale University Press, 1989), 16.

2. Thomas Morley, *A Plain and Easy Introduction to Practical Music* (New York: W. W. Norton & Company, 1973), 9.

3. John Hollander, *The Untuning of the Sky: Ideas of Music in English Poetry, 1500–1700* (New York: W. W. Norton & Company, 1970), 207.

4. Thomson, 32.

Writing [Echoes] Writing

1. Rosmarie Waldrop, *The Reproduction of Profiles* (New York: New Directions, 1987), 13.

2. Wallace Stevens, *The Necessary Angel* (New York: Vintage Books, 1951), 143.

3. Michel Foucault, "What Is an Author?" *The Foucault Reader,* ed. Paul Rabinow (New York: Pantheon Books, 1984), 118–19.

4. Ludwig Wittgenstein, *Zettel* (Berkeley and Los Angeles: University of California Press, 1964), 26e.

5. Wittgenstein, 28e.

6. John Cage, "History of Experimental Music in the United States," *Silence* (Middletown, CT: Wesleyan University Press, 1961), 68.

7. Julia Kristeva, *Desire in Language* (New York: Columbia University Press, 1980), 36.

8. Walter Abish, *99: The New Meaning* (Providence, RI: Burning Deck, 1990), 9.

9. Wittgenstein, 33e.

10. Samuel Beckett, quoted in Marjorie Perloff, *The Poetics of Indeterminancy: Rimbaud to Cage* (Evanston, IL: Northwestern University Press, 1983), 213.

11. Louis Zukofsky, *Catullus (Gai Valeri Catulli Veronensis Liber)* (London: Cape Goliard Press, 1969), n.p.

12. Catullus, *Catullus Tibullus and Pervigilium Veneris* (Cambridge, MA: Harvard University Press, 1968), 33.

13. Ted Berrigan, *The Sonnets* (New York: United Artists Books, 1982), 37.

14. Lyn Hejinian, *My Life* (Los Angeles: Sun & Moon Press, 1987), 27.

15. William Shakespeare, *The Complete Works,* ed. Alfred Harbage (New York: Viking, 1969), 2.3.57–165.

16. Kenneth Koch, *Selected Poems* (New York: Vintage Books, 1985), 51.

17. Ron Padgett, *Tulsa Kid* (Calais, VT: Z Press, 1979) 131.

18. Robert Creeley, "Chasing the Bird," *The Charm* (San Francisco: The Four Seasons Foundation, 1969), 59; "Wall," *Memory Gardens* (New York: New Directions, 1986), 26.

19. Robert Duncan, *Groundwork: Before the War* (New York: New Directions, 1984), 71.

20. Susan Howe, *Articulation of Sound Forms in Time* (Windsor, VT: Awede, 1987), n.p.; reprinted in *Singularities* (Hanover, VT and London: Wesleyan University Press, 1990), 5–6.

21. Howe, *A Bibliography of the King's Book; or, Eikon Basilike,* (Providence, RI: Paradigm Press, 1989), n.p.; reprinted in *The Nonconformist's Memorial* (New York: New Directions, 1993), 68.

22. Anne Waldman, *Helping the Dreamer* (Minneapolis: Coffee House Press, 1989).

23. Charles Bernstein, back cover text for Jackson Mac Low, *Words nd Ends from Ez* (Bolinas, CA: Avenue B, 1989).

24. Jackson Mac Low, *Words nd Ends from Ez* (Bolinas, CA: Avenue B, 1989), 53.

25. Howe, *Singularities,* 42

Notes on Sound

1. Gustaf Sobin, "Road, Roadsides and the Disparate Frames of Sequence," *Temblor* 4 (1986): 3; reprinted in *Voyaging Portraits* (New York: New Directions, 1988), 84.

2. Susan Howe, "Heliopathy," *Temblor* 4 (1986): 43.

3. Howe, "Heliopathy," 43.

4. Ibid.

5. Ibid.

6. Ibid., 42.

7. Stephen Ratcliffe, *[where late the sweet] BIRDS SANG* (Oakland: O Books, 1989), n.p.

8. Howe, "12 poems from a Work in Progress," *Temblor* 3 (1986): 14.

9. Robert Duncan, "Some Notes on Notation," *Groundwork: Before the War* (New York: New Directions, 1984), ix.

10. Leslie Scalapino, *way* (Berkeley: North Point Press, 1988), 41.

11. Victor Zuckerkandl, *Sound and Symbol: Music and the External World* (Princeton: Bollingen Foundation/Princeton University Press, 1956), 371; quoted in Nathaniel Mackey, "Sound and Sentiment, Sound and Symbol," *Callaloo* 10, 1 (Winter 1987): 30.

12. Ezra Pound, *Personae* (New York: New Directions, 1971), 29.

13. Howe, *Articulation of Sound Forms in Time* (Windsor, VT: Awede), n.p.; reprinted in *Singularities* (Hanover, VT and London: Wesleyan University Press, 1990), 11.

14. Claude Royet-Journoud, "A Descriptive Method: Without Any Sound of Syllables," trans. Michael Davidson, *Temblor* 7 (1988): 64–65.

15. William Carlos Williams, *The Collected Poems of William Carlos Williams, Volume 1: 1909–1939,* ed. A. Walton Litz and Christopher MacGowan (New York: New Directions, 1986), 57.

16. Williams, *The Collected Poems of William Carlos Williams, Volume 2: 1939–1962,* ed. Christopher MacGowan (New York: New Directions, 1988), 55.

17. Lorine Niedecker, *The Granite Pail: The Selected Poems of Lorine Niedecker* (Berkeley: North Point Press, 1985), 31.

18. Larry Eigner, *Anything on Its Side* (New Rochelle, NY: Elizabeth Press, 1974), 20.

19. Niedecker, 15.

20. Eigner, 7.

21. Royet-Journoud, "Story in Succession," trans. Michael Davidson, *Temblor* 7 (1988): 67.

22. Sobin, "Seven Entries for a Flora on Speech," *Temblor* 7 (1988): 31; reprinted in *Voyaging Portraits* (New York: New Directions, 1988), 106.

23. Sobin, "Seven Entries for a Flora on Speech," 32; 107.

24. Sobin, "Seven Entries for a Flora on Speech," 33; 108.

25. Sobin, "A Fable for Lighea," *Temblor* 7 (1988): 33; reprinted in *Voyaging Portraits* (New York: New Directions, 1988), 109.

26. Louis Zukofsky, "An Objective," in *Prepositions: The Collected Critical Essays of Louis Zukofsky* (Berkeley and Los Angeles: University of California Press, 1981), 17.

26. Zukofsky, "An Objective," *Preposition* 17.

27. Ibid., 16.

28. Zukofsky, "A Statement for Poetry," *Prepositions,* 19.

29. Zukofsky, "An Objective," 12.

Memo/ Re: Reading Stein

1. Ulla Dydo, ed., *A Stein Reader* (Evanston, IL: Northwestern University Press, 1993), 151. Everything Dydo writes about Stein is worth reading—this, for ex-

ample: "She attempted to work with a sense of language prior to codified syntax and usage in order to recover the sensation of life. As a result, her work sounds and looks unfamiliar and unidiomatic. She forces us to read and see anew with each new piece, sometimes appearing to write in a foreign language which yet turns out to be English. Her language constantly calls attention to itself—to what it is rather than to what it represents. Her word patterns, which do not match our constructive expectations and refuse to be pinned down, appear unstable. Like the glass bits in a kaleidoscope, they constantly move, combining and recombining steadily in new patterns. Since the forms of her work offer no familiar access to the world, they place in doubt the coherence of the world, the authority of language, the possibility of representation." "Reading the Hand Writing: The Manuscripts of Gertrude Stein," *A Gertrude Stein Companion: content with the example,* ed. Bruce Kellner (New York, Westport, CT, London: Greenwood Press, 1988), 84.

2. "Gertrude Stein: Composition as Meditation," *Gertrude Stein and the Making of Literature* ed. Shirley Neuman and Ira B. Nadel (New York: Macmillan Press, 1988) 42.

3. "Words as Pieces Words in Pieces," *West Coast Line: A Journal of Contemporary Writing and Criticism* 3 (1990): 30.

4. Gertrude Stein, "Portraits and Repetition," *Writings and Lectures 1909–1945,* ed. Patricia Meyerowitz (Baltimore: Penguin Books, 1971), 107.

5. Gertrude Stein, "Melanctha," *Three Lives* (New York: Vintage), 394.

6. Dydo, *A Stein Reader,* 568.

7. Stein, "Matisse," *Selected Writings of Gertrude Stein,* ed. Carl van Vechten (New York: Vintage, 1974), 329.

8. Stein, "Tender Buttons," *Selected Writings of Gertrude Stein,* 472.

Writing/ Re: Memory

1. George Lakoff, "On Whose Authority", *Poetry Flash* 147 (June 1985):1.

2. Wallace Stevens, "The House Was Quiet and the World Was Calm," *The Palm at the End of the Mind* (New York: Random House, 1971), 279.

3. Lyn Hejinian, "The Rejection of Closure," *Poetics Journal* 4 (May 1984): 135.

4. Ibid., 136.

5. It is interesting to note that in lines 21–22 these same words reappear spread out over consecutive lines ("Cannot be taught/ and therefore cannot be/ what human cunning can conceal"), where the addition of a complement after the verb *be* invites the reader to an understanding that is entirely different than the one arrived at before. A similar play of elements repeated in different, and difference-making, contexts occurs in lines 11 through 13, where 'whatever interrupts' of line 4 reappears in new form in "Such hopes are set, aroused/ against interruption. Thus—/ in securing sleep against interpretation." Hejinian's account of the effect of this sort of repetition deserves notice: "Repetition, conventionally used to unify a text or harmonize its parts, as if returning melody to the tonic, [here] challenges our inclination to isolate, identify, and limit the burden of meaning given to an event (the sentence or line).

Here, when certain phrases recur in the work, recontextualized and with new emphasis, repetition disrupts the initial apparent meaning scheme. The initial reading is adjusted; meaning is set in motion, emended and extended, and the rewriting that repetition becomes postpones completion of the thought indefinitely ("The Rejection of Closure," 135).

For additional instances of repetition of this sort in part 1 of *The Guard,* see, for example, "Repetition in copying/ seems to mean to say 'I, too'" (lines 31–32); "It takes hollow red & yellow factories" (39) "Memory of a mouth" (42); and "Painting cannot take captives" (67). Consider also the multiple echoes to be found in "Anyone who could believe can reveal it can conceal. A drive of remarks/ and short rejoinders. The seance/ or session. The concentric lapping./ If the world is round" (14–18), and "Resemblance of luggage, and how raw./ How far the length of time it takes./ Repetition in copying/ seems to mean to say 'I, too'// I advise you" (29–33).

6. "The Rejection of Closure," 143.

7. Gertrude Stein, "Portraits and Repetition," *Writing and Lectures 1909–1945,* ed. Patricia Meyerowitz (Baltimore: Penguin Books, 1967), 155. See also "the words that made whatever I looked at look like itself were not the words that had in them any quality of description" (115).

8. "I am always conscious of the disquieting runs of life slipping by, that the message remains undelivered." "Preface," *Writing Is an Aid to Memory* (Great Barrington, MA: The Figures, 1978).

9. "Knowledge is not *translated* into words when it is expressed. The words are not a translation of something else that was there before they were." Ludwig Wittgenstein, *Zettel* (Berkeley and Los Angeles: University of California Press, 1984), 33e.

10. Louis Zukofsky, "The Effacement of Philosophy," *Prepositions* (Berkeley and Los Angeles: University of California Press, 1981), 55.

Grenier's "Scrawl"

1. Louis Zukofsky, "The Effacement of Philosophy," *Prepositions* (Berkeley and Los Angeles: University of California Press, 1981), 55.

2. Robert Grenier, "Interview with Robert Grenier," *The Little Magazine* vol. 20 (1996): 158.

3. Charles Olson, "The Kingfishers," *Selected Writings* (New York: New Directions, 1966), 171.

Listening to Reading

1. Aeolotropy in physics refers to a change in properties consequent upon a change of position.

2. Leslie Scalapino, "Poetic Diaries," *Poetics Journal* 5 (May 1985): 17.

3. Scalapino, 20.

4. Part four of *that they were at the beach,* itself a three-part poem in "notational form" (Scalapino's description of *A Tomb for Anatole,* which work this recalls), is in fact called "chameleon series." Here the counters used to measure out the life reappear again and again, each time in slightly different surroundings, as if seen from a new angle, therefore a new feel and weight. "chameleon series 2" begins:

> There's/ order in/ the goat's// life/—occurring/ later
> on// after that/ life My/ doing so—/ coming/ after// the
> life/ lead/ by the donkey/ Boys and men/ who'd// come/ after
> the// life/ of the goat/ Their/ being mature/ had/ preceded
> there/ being// order/ in the goat's/ life.

Sound (Shape) as Thought

1. In "Composition as Explanation" (*Writings and Lectures 1909–1945,* ed. Patricia Meyerowitz [Baltimore: Penguin Books, 1971]), Stein draws the distinction between time *in* and *of* the "composition"—i.e., the time in which something is written and the time in which events (both verbal and "fictional") unfold within it. See for example the following: "It is understood by this time that everything is the same except composition and time, composition and the time of the composition and the time in the composition" (27–28); "After all this, there is that, there has been that that there is a composition and that nothing changes except composition the composition and the time of and the time in the composition" (29); and "The time of the composition is a natural thing and the time in the composition is a natural thing it is a natural thing and it is a contemporary thing" (29).

2. Stein, 26. "In the first book there was a groping for a continuous present and for using everything by beginning again and again.

"There was a groping for using everything and there was a groping for a continuous present and there was an inevitable beginning of beginning again and again and again."

3. Stein, 26.

4. Louis Zukofsky, "An Objective," *Prepositions* (Berkeley and Los Angeles: University of California Press, 1964), 17.

5. Alan Davies, "U N A D O R N E D ca78," *Signage* (New York: Roof Books, 1987), 55.

6. Quotations in this paragraphs are from *Prepositions:* "A Statement for Poetry," 19; "An Objective," 13; "Ezra Pound," 81.

7. Davies, 57.

8. Zukofsky, "For Wallace Stevens," 33.

9. John Cage, "Lecture on Nothing," *Silence* (Middletown, CT: Wesleyan University Press, 1973), 109.

10. Ibid., 111.

11. Theodor Adorno, *Aesthetic Theory* (London and New York: Routledge & Kegan Paul, 1984), 35.

12. Cage, "45' for a Speaker," *Silence,* 173.

Cracking the Code

1. "Some Fields the Track Goes Through," *L=A=N=G=U=A=G=E* 8 (June 1979), reprinted in *The L=A=N=G=U=A=G=E Book* (Carbondale: Southern Illinois University Press, 1984), 57.

2. "Philosophy & Poetry: A Note," *Poetics Journal* 3 (May 1983): 22–23.

3. "Clark Coolidge, Weathers," *L=A=N=G=U=A=G=E* 12 (June 1980), reprinted in *The L=A=N=G=U=A=G=E Book,* 215.

Supernatural Duet

1. Ted Berrigan, "Interview with Tom Savage," *Talking in Tranquility: Interviews with Ted Berrigan* (Bolinas, CA and Oakland: Avenue B / O Books, 1991), 162, 163–64.

2. Ibid., 162.

Index